W9-CMN-082

J
613.
7
Sch
Schwarzenegger, Arnold.
    Arnold's fitness for
    kids ages 6 to 10
    c1993 $15.00
    0002200488324 BE

CASS COUNTY PUBLIC LIBRARY
400 E. MECHANIC
HARRISONVILLE, MO 64701

1-18-94
BE

arnold's fitness for kids

ages 6–10

doubleday

new york

london

toronto

sydney

auckland

arnold's fitness for kids

ages 6–10
a guide to health, exercise, and nutrition

arnold schwarzenegger
with charles gaines

CASS COUNTY PUBLIC LIBRARY
400 E. MECHANIC

4701

0 0022 0048832 4

BE

illustrations by jackie aher
and denise donnell

Handlettering and endpaper design by Robert de Michiell

published by doubleday
a division of Bantam Doubleday Dell Publishing Group, Inc.
666 Fifth Avenue, New York, New York 10103

doubleday and the portrayal of an anchor with a
dolphin are trademarks of Doubleday, a division of
Bantam Doubleday Dell Publishing Group, Inc.

Book design by Marysarah Quinn and Claire N. Vaccaro

Library of Congress Cataloging-in-Publication Data
Schwarzenegger, Arnold.
  [Fitness for kids ages 6–10]
  Arnold's fitness for kids ages 6–10 : a guide to health,
exercise, and nutrition / Arnold Schwarzenegger with Charles Gaines.
      p.   cm.
  Includes bibliographical references.
  Summary: Discusses fitness, nutrition, and exercise and suggests
exercises and other activities for both active children
and those less athletically inclined.
    1. Physical fitness for children.   [1. Physical fitness.   2. Exercise.
3. Nutrition.]   I. Gaines, Charles, 1942–
II. Title.   III. Title: Fitness for kids ages 6 to 10.
GV443.S38   1993
613.7′042—dc20   92-28577
                                                              CIP
                                                              AC

ISBN 0-385-42267-9

Copyright © 1993 by Fitness Publications, Inc.

All Rights Reserved
Printed in the United States of America
April 1993

10 9 8 7 6 5 4 3 2 1

First Edition

To Charles Gaines, his wife
Patricia, and their children
Latham, Greta, and Shelby,
who show how a family can
spiritedly and joyfully join
together to make sports and
fitness a crucial, enduring,
and wonderful part of
their lives.
—Arnold Schwarzenegger

To the memory of
Naomi Weiss.
—Charles Gaines

This series is also dedicated
to the world's children with
the wish that we could give
every one of them the
priceless gift of lifelong
fitness and good health.
—Arnold Schwarzenegger
and Charles Gaines

Contents

INTRODUCTION

a note to parents from arnold

There is nothing more precious in life to parents than the health and happiness of their children. I hope that by reading this book, you will be on your way to making a major contribution to the lifetime health and happiness of your child. At the same time, you will help me to turn around a fitness crisis in this country among our young people.

As I travel around the country in my position as chairman of the President's Council on Physical Fitness and Sports, I am constantly astounded by how little parents are concerned about the fitness levels of their children, and by the general lack of information available on the importance of youth fitness. I've had dozens of mothers and fathers walk up to me and say things like, "Of course my little Tommy is fit—he's a child, isn't he?" or "Well, maybe Debbie is obese, but she'll grow out of it, and anyway, it won't affect her health at this age," or "Sure my twins, Jim and Judy, spend all their free time watching TV and eating junk food, but they're only eight years old—they'll get plenty of exercise when they get into high school."

I have written this book with my friend Charles Gaines to correct some of that misinformation, and to encourage parents like you to join with me in a crusade to make American young people fit again.

Now, you might be one of those parents I meet on the road who wonder why it *is* so important for kids to be fit—particularly kids as young as ages six through ten. Well, the short answer to that question is that both the length and the quality of your child's life depend on it.

Fitness, after all, is just another word for good health, and chances are that unfit kids are less healthy than fit ones and will remain so later on in life.

As Bob Glover and Jack Shepherd write in *The Family Fitness Handbook,* "Kids who are physically fit are at lower risk for hypokinetic diseases such as hypertension, cardiovascular disease, tension syndromes, diabetes, gastrointestinal disease (ulcers—yes, our high-stress kids get ulcers), and emotional problems. *These degenerative diseases all begin in childhood.*" (Italics mine.)

Of the potential liabilities of poor fitness among kids, the most serious is heart disease, which is the leading cause of death and disability in America. If you think heart disease has nothing to do with childhood, think again. According to the *Research Quarterly,* "It is well established that atherosclerotic heart disease begins at an early age and available evidence suggests that physical activity in children is inversely associated with other coronary risk factors." And Dr. Elvin Smith of the Texas A&M College of Medicine writes, "Much of heart disease can be traced to having its initiation in early childhood. If nothing more is done, we'll continue to see a gradual slip in fitness and kids will have a difficult time making any impact on heart disease. It makes little sense to invest in a child's education and leave him at risk for heart disease."

But maybe you are one of those nine out of ten parents who think that risk doesn't apply to you because *your* kid is in great shape and gets plenty of exercise. The chances are excellent you're dead wrong. The fact is that kids across the board are fatter and less fit than they were fifteen years ago, including, very possibly, your own. Just look at a few of these statistics:

► **Obesity among children six to eleven has increased by 54 percent since the 1960s, according to a 1987 study conducted by the Harvard School of Public Health.**

► **Only 32 percent of children ages six to seventeen meet *minimum* standards for cardiovascular fitness, flexibility, and abdominal and upper-body strength, according to a 1989 AAU study of twelve thousand youths. (In 1981, 43 percent of the children were in acceptable shape.)**

► **A horrifying *40 percent* of American children five to eight have at least one heart-disease risk factor, according to the President's Council on Physical Fitness and Sports.**

► **Only *one* state, Illinois, has a mandatory daily physical education requirement for all students, kindergarten through high school.**

Here's the bottom line, parents: *the great majority of our kids are physically unfit; those kids are on a fast track to becoming unhealthy adults; and the situation is getting worse rather than better.* As my friend Dr. Kenneth Cooper has summed it up in his book *Kid Fitness,* "Millions of our children—the majority of them in middle- and upper-middle-class homes—face the prospect of serious disease and shortened lifespans because of sedentary living and poor nutrition."

That's the bad news. The good news is that together with your child, you can work (and play) to help him or her build a solid fitness foundation for a lifetime of good health.

If extended good health is the biggest package under the Christmas tree of childhood fitness, there are many other presents there as well. Fit kids are happier kids. They have better posture, sleep and move better, recover more quickly from sickness and injury, have more endurance and concentration, and can handle physical emergencies more easily than unfit kids. As you will learn in this book, exercise plays a key role in helping young people develop important motor skills such as agility, coordination, and balance. Exercise also helps keep fat off kids, improving health and making movement easier and more efficient. I have always felt that exercise is tremendously important in boosting self-esteem among young people, and recent studies by child fitness expert Dr. Charles Kuntzleman and others bear this out. When I was a kid, exercise made me feel great about myself. And finally, but by no means least, there's considerable evidence—including a six-year Canadian study—to show that exercise improves academic performance.

Let me ask you this: if there was something you could go out and buy for your child that would make him far healthier, happier, and better prepared to deal with life than he would be without this thing, wouldn't you sell whatever you had to sell, do whatever you had to do, to get it? Well, there is such a thing—fitness. I believe it is the most valuable gift you can give your child.

family fitness

This is a book for kids six through ten years old *and their parents*. No fitness program for kids this age could possibly work without the commitment and involvement of you, the parent. I know you're busy. So am I. But I find at least thirty minutes every day to play and exercise with my two daughters, and so can you. When you think about it, what could you possibly be doing for that half hour to an hour each day that is more important?

Besides, family fitness is wonderful fun, and it provides unique opportunities for developing closer relationships with your kids.

A 1988 study by the widely respected Melpomene Institute showed that the most important influences on a child's involvement in physical activity and exercise are: (1) the parents' physical activity habits; (2) lessons, classes, and recreation programs in the community; and

(3) the time parents spend with the child exercising and doing physical activities.

In Chapter 4 of this book, I discuss the important role that schools should play in your child's fitness life, and Chapter 5 is given over to community programs. But most of this book deals with family fitness and that is as it should be, since fitness, like charity, truly begins at home.

"The best and easiest way to motivate your child to stay fit is to stay fit yourself," writes child and adolescent psychiatrist Dr. Paul H. Gabriel. "The main reason children are out of shape is that they

have poor role models. By making fitness a part of your life, you teach your child to value it."

This information should be self-evident, but too often it is not. In fact, the National Children and Youth Fitness Study II found that very few parents set good fitness examples for their kids: nearly half of all parents of young children *never* exercise vigorously, and less than 30 percent get the recommended minimum level of exercise per week. What you do or don't do *counts* with your kids. It is almost impossible to convince children not to drink and smoke if you do those things yourself. Similarly, you'll be much more effective in getting your child to become conscious of what and how he eats if you're not always pigging out on doughnuts, and more successful in getting him away from the TV to exercise if you're not always there beside him on the couch.

So my first words of advice to you as a parent about to encourage your child to become and stay fit are these: *Practice what you preach.* Make yourself a living example of the lifetime benefits of fitness.

My second suggestion is: *Do physical activities and exercises with your kids.* For parents of kids in the six-to-ten age range, this is crucially important advice. Dr. Paul Dyment, chairman of the Sports Medicine Committee of the American Academy of Pediatrics, advises: "By the time a child is five the whole family should be regularly doing something to-

gether, say walking or biking, so that the child grows up with physical activity as part of its culture."

There are two ways for you and your child to exercise and be physically active together: you can involve the child in your own exercise programs (for example, I encourage my older daughter, Catherine, to do calisthenics with me); or you can join into and find ways to extend your child's exercise and play—play hide-and-seek or tag; roll around on the grass; wrestle on the bed. I recommend you do them all. And don't tell me you don't have the time. *Make* the time. In Chapter 2, I give a list of tips for making fitness an organic, enjoyable part of life with your kids. If you follow these tips, I guarantee you that your child will grow up loving exercise and physical activity.

My final suggestion is this: *Make fitness fun.* If you make exercise and good nutrition seem like homework, your kids will run the opposite way every time they see you coming. I can promise you that. The fact is that using and exercising our bodies and nourishing them well *are* fun—the greatest fun there is, I believe—you just have to find ways to demonstrate that fun

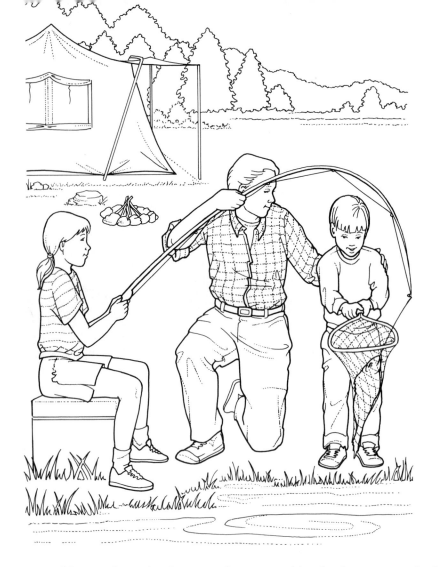

to your kids. Forget about getting them to exercise because it is "good for them"; that will never work. What does work is to make your family play and exercise sessions imaginative and enjoyable. Do that and your kids will run to them rather than away from them.

how you should use this book

This book has been conceived and written to be user friendly for you and your child. This is not a fitness textbook, full of charts and tables and medical terms, but a workbook that can and should be used by parents and kids together.

In order to help the book appeal directly to your kids, and to entice them to pick it up and use it, I have written a little series of children's stories about myself as a child growing up in Austria, living an energetic, physically active life with my family and friends. These stories are interspersed between the book's chapters, and may be read separately as individual stories relating to fitness and good health, or together as a small children's book.

Chapter 1 is a discussion of what fitness is and how it applies to kids at this age level. I discuss the significance of each of the categories of health-related fitness—aerobic, or heart/lung, endurance capacity; flexibility; muscular strength and stamina; and body-fat percentage—and explain how each is relevant to kids ages six through ten. Then I discuss the importance of "motor," or physical, skills, such as balance, agility, and hand-eye coordination. These skills are not only a prerequisite for performing well at sports, but provide kids with a good "movement base" from which they can effectively take up a wide range of fitness and recreational activities throughout their lives. I encourage you to read this chapter to or with your child. There is good, simply stated information on how the body works and on the relationship of exercise to good health and good performance.

Chapter 2 explains how to put together your own family fitness program for getting your child in great shape. Again, I suggest that you read this chapter together with your child or children; then as a group, all of you design your own "family program" and then make it happen. Also in this chapter I'll tell you how to create "fitness days," "fitness weekends," "Backyard Olympics," and "fitness vacations" for your kids, and how to throw great "fitness parties."

Chapters 3 through 5 are for parents (though some kids might want to read them too), and contain information you'll need to be a good fitness parent. Chapter 3 is a guide to smart and healthful eating. Chapter 4 focuses on the role the schools play, or should play, in your child's fitness life. It gives you recommended school physical education standards and tells you how to lobby with other parents for improvement if those standards are not being met, as too often they are not. Chapter 5 deals with community programs and camps that can extend physical activity and fitness options for your child beyond school and the home and takes a look at the role organized sports can play in developing and sustaining your child's physical fitness.

As I said earlier, this is not a high-tech fitness book. You'll find no complicated tests here to determine how your child fits in to national body-fat percentage tables; no calorie-counting menus for eight-year-olds; and no traditional "exercise programs." These days, what parent has time to read all that stuff, or do the testing, or count the calories? I certainly don't, and I'm sure you don't either. The truth is fitness is commonsense eating and exercise, and you don't need a lot of tables and tests to tell you how to do that. Back in Austria when I was growing up, *everyone* was fit, kids and adults alike. We ate good, healthful, homemade food and got plenty of exercise as a normal part of our lives, both playing and working. Being in good physical shape was just a natural and joyous result of the family life we lived. And that's what I want to see us get back to here in this country.

One of my colleagues commented recently on the sad state of American youth fitness: "Arnold, we are raising a generation of heart patients." Well, not if I can help it, we're not. Our kids' health is our future, and ensuring that future is the ultimate responsibility of each and every one of us as parents. This particular buck doesn't stop with the government or the community or the schools, but right in the home with you and me. *Now* is the time to start turning things around. So, welcome aboard—and let's get going.

FITNESS

what is physical fitness?

The American Alliance of Health, Physical Education, Recreation and Dance (AAHPERD) defines physical fitness as: *"A physical state of well-being that allows people to perform daily activities with vigor, reduce their risk of health problems related to lack of exercise, and to establish a fitness base for participation in a variety of physical activities."*

That's a good definition. But what does it mean for *you?* First of all, the definition says that fitness is a "state of well-being." That means that you feel good when you're fit, that you're happy. I can tell you that I'm happy and feel good all the time because I'm fit.

Second, the definition says that being fit lets you "perform daily activities with vigor." That simply means you have more energy for school and play and all the other things you do in your life.

Next, according to the definition, fitness reduces your "risk of health problems related to lack of exercise." If you are fit, in other words, you are less likely to get sick, both while you're young and when you get older.

And finally, the definition says that fitness lets you establish a "base for participation in a variety of physical activities." That means that when you are fit you are prepared to learn to do a lot of fun things with your body—from sports like baseball and soccer and field hockey, to dancing and ice skating and hiking and skateboarding, and all sorts of other things, even flying an airplane. So, in a nutshell, what fitness means to you is that when you are fit you feel good, you have plenty of energy, you are healthy, and you can learn to do all sorts of interesting new things with your body. Your body is your good friend when you are fit—a healthy, happy friend that will do whatever you want it to do. Fit is the only way I want to be, and I'm sure it's the way you want to be too.

fitness for good health

You can be "physically fit" for a lot of different things. You can be physically fit to sit in a chair all day, but that doesn't mean you're physically fit to climb a mountain. You can be physically fit to hit a baseball a long way, but have to huff and puff your way around the bases. What I care about most is that you are physically fit *to be healthy*. We call that kind of fitness "health-related physical fitness," and there are four parts to it. To be physically fit for good health:

1. Your heart and lungs should be strong and efficient.

2. Your joints and muscles should be flexible.

3. Your muscles should be strong and have endurance.

4. You shouldn't be overly fat.

Now let's take a look at each one of those four parts, and see what it has to do with your health.

heart/lung strength

Did you know that your heart is a muscle? Yes—the most important one in your body. The heart is a muscle that works all the time pumping blood through your body. The normal heart "beats," or contracts, about one hundred thousand times a day, pumping more than a gallon of blood per minute through thousands of miles of arteries and veins. And that's just when the heart is taking it easy! When you are exercising, it can beat more than twice as fast and can pump *five or six times* more blood. Like any muscle, the heart loves to work, and it gets bigger and stronger (and healthier) with the right kind of exercise.

The right kind of exercise for the heart is called "aerobic" exercise, which means exercise that requires a lot of oxygen from the body over an extended time and that improves the body's ability to handle and transport oxygen.

All muscles need oxygen to work, or exercise, and the harder they work, the more oxygen they need. The muscles get oxygen like this: every time you take a breath, air is drawn into millions of little air sacs in the lungs. Those little sacs load oxygen onto the red blood cells as your blood courses through the wall of each sac. You can think of the sacs as loading depots, and the red blood cells as tiny train cars picking up the oxygen in the sacs and carrying it to your muscles. As a muscle or group of muscles begins to work, or exercise, it needs more oxygen than usual and the body supplies that extra oxygen in two ways: the lungs begin to draw in more air, sending more oxygen into the air sacs for delivery, and the heart begins to pump faster, sending more blood through the lungs. With the lungs and the heart both working harder, there is more oxygen in the depots ready for delivery, and more train cars going through the depots to pick up the oxygen for delivery to the muscles. The next time you're exercising, when your heart begins to beat faster and you start to pant, think of how your heart and lungs are working together to load oxygen and hurry it to your muscles.

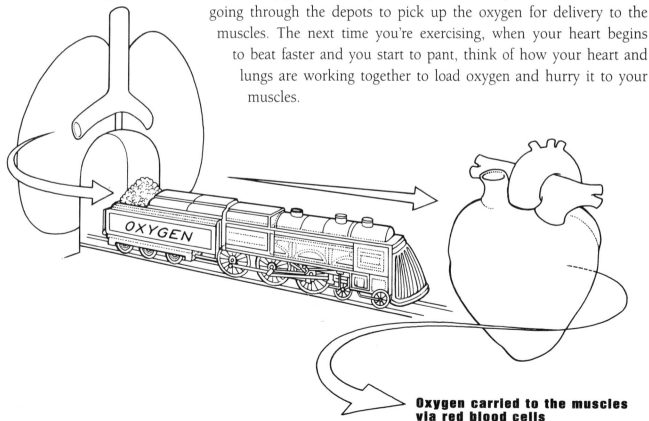

Oxygen carried to the muscles via red blood cells

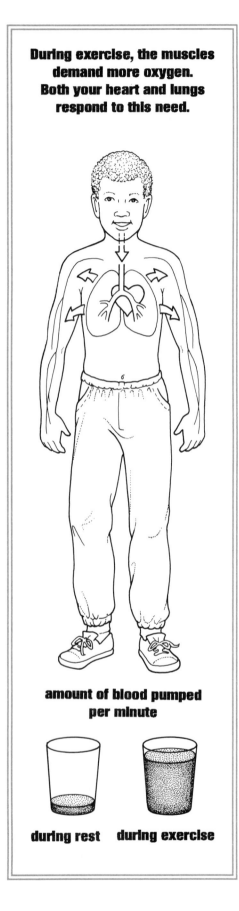

During exercise, the muscles demand more oxygen. Both your heart and lungs respond to this need.

amount of blood pumped per minute

during rest   during exercise

The more your heart and lungs and blood-carrying system work together in this way, the better able they are to do it, and the healthier they are. Also, research shows that regular exercise that forces your heart and lungs to work hard together over a period of time (aerobic exercise) can help you avoid heart disease, as well as many other ailments.

There are many kinds of exercise that help strengthen your heart and lungs and make them work better together. Some of those exercises are walking, running, biking, swimming, cross-country skiing, rowing, and climbing up mountains. There are also lots of games that improve aerobic fitness. In the next chapter, I'll talk more about those games and exercises, and in Appendix A of this book is a list of them for you to choose from in putting together your fitness program.

joint and muscle flexibility

Flexibility is the ability to move your muscles and joints smoothly and fully. Every joint—such as the elbow, knee, back, and hip—has an ideal "range of motion." If your knee, for example, can move smoothly throughout its entire range of motion, it has good flexibility. If it can only move through part of its range of motion, your knee's flexibility is not as good as it should be.

Flexible joints and muscles are less prone to injury than stiff ones, and that is why they are healthier.

Think about it this way: flexible joints and muscles are like strands of cooked spaghetti—you can twist and turn and fold them without breaking or tearing them. Stiff muscles and joints are more like *uncooked* pieces of spaghetti—you can't bend them much without damaging them.

Most of us are born with very good flexibility in our joints and muscles, but we can lose that flexibility quickly through inactivity. Even kids between six and ten often have stiff joints and muscles that are not as flexible as they should be. Flexibility not only helps prevent injury, but it also allows you to do many things more easily and better, including a lot of sports, such as gymnastics, swimming, tennis, and skateboarding. Dancers have to be very flexible too. Good flexibility in all your joints and muscles allows you to move your body easily, gracefully, and injury-free through hundreds of activities.

Every joint has an ideal "range of motion."

Many, many American adults have lower back pain. Often that pain could have been avoided if the people suffering from it had done exercises to keep their back joints and muscles flexible.

Stretching is the type of exercise we use to keep muscles and joints flexible, as well as to warm up for aerobic exercise and to cool down after it. In the next chapter, I will tell you more about how and when to do stretching exercises, and at the end of the book, I'll show you a number of good stretches to use in your exercise program.

muscle strength and endurance

Everybody knows that it is better to have strong muscles than weak ones —and that goes for *girls* as well as boys. It is also *healthier* to have strong muscles, because they are like the body's armor protecting us from injury. Strong muscles can also prevent people from developing back, neck, and other problems. Despite living a very active physical life, I have never had a serious injury, and I know that is partly because all my life my muscles have been strong.

The strength of a muscle is the ability to exert force over a short period of time. Muscle endurance is the muscle's ability to do something over and over again without tiring out. Both muscle strength and muscle endurance are important to your health.

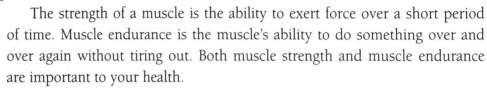

They are also important for playing sports, and for doing many things in everyday life. Many sports require good muscle endurance, and some sports —like weightlifting, the field events, football, rowing, and gymnastics—require considerable strength as well. Muscular strength and the ability of muscles to work for long periods of time without tiring out are useful not only to athletes, but to carpenters, dancers, furniture movers, woodsmen, construction workers, firemen—all kinds of people who work and play with their bodies.

Muscles are made strong, and build endurance, by working or exercising them *against* something. This kind of exercise is known as resistance exercise. When you do a push-up, your chest, shoulder, and arm muscles are working against the resistance of your own body. Weightlifters and bodybuilders work their muscles against the resistance of the barbells and dumbbells they lift. In the next chapter, I'll tell you how to exercise your muscles against the resistance of your own body in order to make them strong and develop endurance, and at the end of the book I'll show you some muscle-strengthening exercises.

fat versus lean

Our bodies are composed of "fat weight," which is made up of fatty tissue, and "lean weight," which is made up of the body's internal organs, bone, and muscle tissue. To be physically fit for good health, you shouldn't have too high a percentage of fat weight. According to Dr. Kenneth Cooper, in boys between five and eighteen, the optimal range of body-fat percentage is between 10 percent and 20 percent. In girls of the same age, the optimal range is between 15 percent and 25 percent. A body-fat percentage that is too high is known as obesity, and obesity has been associated by doctors with high blood pressure, heart disease, and many other health problems.

It is a lot of extra work for the body to carry fat around because, unlike muscle, fat doesn't pull its own weight. Bodies that have to lug around a lot of useless fat are not as healthy as lean bodies. They usually can't perform as well at sports, and they have to work harder at all the physical movements of day-to-day living.

If you want to find out how fat you are, a bathroom scale can't really tell you. Because muscle and bone are heavier than fat, it is possible for you to be heavy on the scale and yet lean, or to be light on the scale and yet too fat.

The best and healthiest way to control your body-fat percentage is through a combination of sensible eating and exercise. Fat is produced when the body is taking in and holding on to more calories than it needs. Sensible, healthful eating can control the number of calories you are taking in, and exercise can help burn off whatever calories you don't need. If you eat smart and get plenty of exercise, you'll never have to worry about being too fat.

Now that we've reviewed the four parts of physical fitness for good health, you can see the one thing that they all have in common is exercise. In fact, regular exercise and eating sensibly are the two keys to health-related physical fitness—both for adults and for kids. As Dr. Mike Samuels and Nancy Samuels write in *The Well Child Book*: "Children who exercise regularly will be *stronger, more flexible, thinner, have greater aerobic power*, and *have larger muscle and bones* than similar children who do not exercise regularly." (Italics mine.)

fitness for physical skills

As I said before, you can be physically fit for many different things. Do you remember the example of the kid who could hit a baseball a long way but who couldn't run around the bases without huffing and puffing? Well, that would be a kid who was "physically fit" for the skill of hitting a baseball (which is a hard thing to do), but who had poor "aerobic," or heart/lung, fitness.

As we've already seen, the most important kind of physical fitness is that directly related to good health, but there is another kind of fitness that is almost as important: *fitness for the performance of physical skills.*

Physical, or "motor," skills are the building blocks of bodily movement. Every coordinated movement that we make with our bodies is based on a motor skill, or a number of motor skills put together. We begin acquiring motor skills from the moment we are born, and those early skills—such as grasping, reaching, sucking—become the first building blocks for all our future movements.

More primary motor skills are acquired during the first two years of life than at any other time, and many experts believe that *all* the primary motor skills a person will ever have are acquired by age ten. (According to these experts, all skills acquired after age ten are modifications and new combinations of the primary skills you already have.) Children who are encouraged or stimulated by their parents to learn new physical skills when they are very young will almost always acquire *more* skills and acquire them *faster* than children who are not encouraged to do so. (For more on this, see my book *Arnold's Fitness for Kids Ages Birth–5*.)

Why are motor skills so important? Simply because they form the foundation of all your physical activity for the rest of your life. There are many, many adult Americans who are physically inactive because as children they never acquired the skills that would have allowed them to participate in and enjoy sports and other physical activities. In this way, motor skills have quite a lot to do with health-related fitness, because you have to have a good skills base in order to perform many health-related fitness activities and exercises.

Professor Vern Seefeldt, director of the Youth Sports Institute at Michigan State University, has written, "The focus of children's fitness should be on developing motor skills. Running, hopping, jumping, skipping, throwing, catching, and kicking are the ABC's of movement. We found that when children have these skills, fitness and sports are second nature. Most children just haven't mastered movement, and so they are reluctant to move."

If a good skills foundation is important to the performance of health-related fitness activities and exercise, it is absolutely crucial to the performance and enjoyment of sports. No one enjoys doing things they cannot do well, and that is particularly true of sports. If you start playing baseball with some of your friends and find out you can't bat or catch or throw well, the chances are good you won't play baseball for very long, and you will probably never come back to it later on in your life. If you begin playing baseball with good throwing, catching, and batting skills, however, you will perform better at the sport, enjoy it more, and very likely stay with it.

The development of physical skills has considerable importance in areas other than sports and fitness. Good motor skills are necessary in activities as various as flying an airplane, ballet dancing, sculpting, typing, and surgery. With well-developed physical skills, you can go through life able to do things, athletic and otherwise, that require coordination and grace. You can enjoy your body and take pleasure in the wonderful variety of movements it is capable of.

In Chapter 2, I will tell you more about motor skills and how to develop them, and in Appendix B, you'll find lots of fun "skill drills" and games to help you develop and improve your physical skills for fitness, sports, and everyday life.

fitness for fun

For me the things most fun in life are physical things—skiing, lifting weights, tennis, hiking. I love to do all those activities and lots of others as well, and so do my family and friends. Those are the things we have fun doing, so we keep ourselves fit to do them—fit while having fun.

Fitness isn't like taking medicine—it's simply living in such a way that enables you to develop a body strong, flexible, and healthy enough to do all the things in life you wish to do.

When I was growing up in Austria, my friends and I exercised all the time without even knowing it was exercise. We walked or rode our bikes to and from school; we played soccer and other games outside with our parents every afternoon; and on weekends we went skiing, or hiking, or mountain climbing, or swimming in the lake. We didn't think of ourselves as being physically fit, but we were. We were just living and enjoying a life of good food and plenty of exercise that made us, and kept us, able to do all the fun things we wanted to do.

And that's what I want for you—the fun and good health of a physically active life. And I want exercise to become as normal and enjoyable and necessary in your life as it was and still is in mine.

So let's go on now to the next chapter and see how to do that.

family

2 making fitness a part of your family life

I. a few notes for parents on your child's fitness development

The last chapter outlined what physical fitness means for young people. As we have seen, what is most important is that your child becomes physically fit for a lifetime of good health with the right kind of exercise and sensible nutrition. It is also very important that your children—boys and girls—develop, by the time they are ten years old, a good broad base of fundamental physical skills,

ones that will give them access for the rest of their lives to sports, fitness activities, and the pleasures of efficient physical movement. Later in this chapter we will see how to put those principles into practice by forming programs that combine health-related and skill-related activities and exercises. But first, let's look at exactly what your goals should be as your child develops from ages six through ten.

You will see that there are two different sets of programs recommended here—one for six- and seven-year-olds, and one for kids eight through ten. I will explain why we make this division where we do, but it is important for you to remember that children develop physically at different speeds and that chronological age is just a general and often inexact marker of developmental stages. In other words, your child might be a little late or early with any of the developmental averages discussed here and yet be perfectly normal and healthy. If you have a seven-year-old who really wants to make his muscles stronger, let him try some of the exercises in the calisthenic strength program recommended here for children ages eight through ten. Or if you have an eight-year-old who doesn't seem ready for that program, drop it and substitute more flexibility or skills training. The point is you don't want to push a child to do any more than he or she is capable of, or wants to do, at a particular stage of development, but neither do you want to hold an enthusiastic child back unnecessarily. The age guidelines given here are just that—general guidelines. You are the best judge of how they apply to your child.

ages six and seven

"These years," says Dr. Kenneth Cooper in his book *Kid Fitness,* "may be absolutely pivotal for the future fitness and athletic endeavors of many children."

Why? Because, though most kids who drop out of fitness activities and sports for good do so from about age eight through early adolescence, it is often during these six to eight years that they form the *attitudes* toward exercise and sports that will lead them to decide whether to stick with it or not. So it is doubly important during these years that (1) *fitness be perceived by kids as fun and stress-free; (2) that they be allowed to develop physically at their own pace;* and (3) *that they encounter nothing but support and encouragement from parents during that development.*

Boys and girls stay about equal physiologically during this period, so it is fine for them to compete against one another and play together. However, the organs and bones in kids of this age are still far from mature and are susceptible to injury, so care should be taken that six- and seven-year-olds compete and roughhouse only with kids at a similar stage of physical development, regardless of chronological age. Also, though kids of this age can safely participate in vigorous sports, you should keep them out of high-impact contact sports such as football, hockey, and lacrosse.

It is in this age range that many kids first become interested in organized team sports such as community league T-ball and soccer, and such sports programs can be excellent for building skills and getting kids turned on to exercise. But parents need to make sure that the sports and organized group play programs their kids enter at this tender point in their lives stress the proper things—fun, general participation, and performance approval—without putting too much emphasis on winning. Again, if you want to cut the chances of your child's suddenly and permanently "dropping out" of exercise and sports later on, you should do everything you can to make his first experience with those things as enjoyable, stress-free, and ego-building as possible.

Most kids in the six-through-seven age range don't yet have problems with flexibility, but some basic stretching is appropriate for them before and after aerobic exercise and games. Though both boys and girls can increase muscular strength and endurance during these years, I don't recommend muscle-strengthening exercises yet for two reasons: the fitness benefits of increased strength at this age are minimal; and most kids this age don't enjoy resistance exercise. In exercises like gymnastics and tumbling, kids are getting muscle-strengthening benefits anyway by using their own body weight.

Remember, *enjoyment* is the key word here. Exercise for a six- or seven-year-old *has* to be fun, or he or she simply won't do it for long, no matter how persuasive you are. This is especially true with aerobic exercise. Even many adults, after all, find running laps boring. Six- and seven-year-olds can get plenty of benefit from aerobic exercise, but to get that benefit they have to exercise regularly, and to exercise regularly they have to enjoy it. Some kids *will* enjoy doing one or more of the traditional aerobic exercises (walking, running, swimming, biking) with you; for those who don't, aerobic games and play are a good substitute.

According to some experts, the most important single thing you can do for your child's physical fitness at this age is to make certain that his or her motor skills are being well developed and refined. Ages six and seven are crucial skills development years, and the more skills your child masters now, the easier and more enjoyable *all* fitness and sports activities will be for him later on. Luckily, most kids *do* enjoy the skill exercises I've included in this book.

As the parent of a six- or seven-year-old who wants that child to be physically fit for good health and to have every opportunity to achieve his full physical and athletic potential, your objectives should be to make exercise and the acquisition of new physical skills as necessary and normal a part of your child's life as brushing his teeth or eating; and to make it *all* fun, all of the time. Within that context, physical fitness for kids at this age is really about three things:

▶ **Good nutrition**

▶ **Getting a minimum of fifteen minutes of aerobic exercise or play at least three days a week**

▶ **Developing and improving motor skills**

And in Part II of this chapter I'll show you and your child how to build a program centered around those priorities.

ages eight, nine, and ten

Experts believe that it is somewhere around eight years of age that most kids first develop an awareness of how they perform physically in comparison with other children. That is a big milestone, marking the beginning of physical self-consciousness—the beginning of a child feeling either shame or pride in how he is able to do things with his body—and that beginning can determine the rest of a person's physical life.

Dr. Kenneth Cooper calls these years the Early Team Phase, because over 80 percent of kids in this age range participate in some form of community-sponsored physical activity, usually a team sport, and many kids are also becoming engaged for the first time in school team sports and competitions. For some kids, those who enter this phase with an already well-developed base of motor skills, a competitive personality, a lucky set of hereditary attributes, or all three, the Early Team Phase can be a picnic. But for other kids, it can be a nightmare of taunts ("You're the worst hitter on the team"; "Even Larry's a better goalie than you are") and embarrassments. It is usually these kids who make up the first big wave of dropouts from sports (subsequent waves account for an estimated 80 to 90 percent of *all* children dropping out of organized sports by age fifteen or sixteen), and too often from all forms of fitness-oriented exercise.

As the parents of a child who is eight, nine, or ten years old, you must do what you can to insure that whatever disillusionment your child might suffer through his first exposure to organized sports doesn't carry over to the rest of his physical life. The best ways to do this are: (1) *carefully monitor the kind of competitive programs your child enters in the community and school, and keep up with the effect that they are having on him;* and (2) *make sure your family fitness activities are kept noncompetitive and fun, and that they constantly build up your child's self-esteem.*

Girls and boys in this age range still remain about the same physically, and can continue to compete and play together more or less evenly. The bone-growth plates of both boys and girls are still open and vulnerable to injury, and high-impact sports such as football and hockey should still be avoided. Kids this age should have strength training (and most of them are now old enough to begin to enjoy it as well as to benefit from it), but I recommend the kind of calisthenic exercises described in Part II of this chapter for that training, rather than weights.

Many kids in this age range have already begun to lose some joint and muscle flexibility, so stretching exercises are recommended.

Kids eight through ten should be getting twenty minutes of aerobic exercise three days a week, but as with the six- and seven-year-olds, this exercise *has* to be made fun. If your child enjoys walking, running, swimming, or biking with you, fine; if not, sugarcoat the pill in aerobic games and play.

Skills development and refinement are still tremendously important up through the age of ten, and even though kids will now be getting some practice at skills in school and through organized sports, it is advisable to supplement and vary that practice at home with exercises and games.

Before we go on to the details of how to put together a family fitness program, here are two very important medical notes:

1. Before starting on a fitness program with your child, if you have been physically inactive for any period of time and/or are over forty years of age, get a check-up from your doctor and discuss with him the exercise program you're beginning. You should also check with your family doctor or pediatrician before starting your child on an exercise program, particularly if the child is overweight.

2. Children produce more body heat during exercise than adults do and have less efficient mechanisms for dispelling that heat. *Always* encourage your kids to drink plenty of water before and during exercise, particularly in hot weather, and make certain that they don't become overheated during exercise.

Just as it is with the younger kids, the key to creating a family fitness program for eight- through ten-year-olds is to make exercise and motor skills development normal and necessary parts of your family life. The fitness priorities around which you'll build your family program for kids this age are:

▶ **Good nutrition**

▶ **Twenty minutes of aerobic exercise or play three days a week**

▶ **Some flexibility and strength training**

▶ **Developing and refining motor skills**

II. putting together your family fitness program

Okay, kids and parents, before we start getting fit, I want to repeat something I've already said, because it's so important: IN ORDER FOR A FITNESS PROGRAM TO WORK FOR YOU, YOU HAVE TO MAKE IT A NORMAL AND NECESSARY PART OF YOUR FAMILY LIFE.

I've made up a list of fifteen tips to help you do that.

arnold's tips for family fitness

▶ First of all, parents and kids should make a deal with one another (draw it up as a contract, if you want to) obligating themselves to get in shape and stay in shape together. Nobody is going to miss a workout. *Ever!*

▶ Pick a time every day to do your program, and stick to it. Give that time of day over to exercising together no matter what, the same way you'd give over the dinner hour to eating together.

▶ Speaking of eating, make smart eating a part of your family life *now*. My chapter on nutrition will give you some good tips on how to do that.

▶ Limit your TV watching. It robs the whole family of time you could be spending together having fun and exercising. In my family, we limit TV time to five hours a week, and we all choose together what those five hours will be. Also, don't put a TV in your kid's room, and encourage him not to watch television until his academic and physical education is done each day.

► Set individual fitness goals for yourselves (one child's goal might be to do ten push-ups by June; a parent's goal might be to start jogging), and help each other to realize those goals. Keep written records of your exercise programs and the goals you've reached, and reward each other with prizes.

► Join a family exercise or fitness club—a YMCA or a racquet club—that the whole family can go to for swimming, racquet sports, aerobic classes, wally-ball, etc.

► When you exercise together, do it at the level of the least skilled, youngest, or least fit member of your family. Set fun competitions within the family in games and sports, but only ones where nobody really loses. And stress "personal best"—each family member competing against himself or herself to improve individual performance levels.

► Create a sense of pride around your being a "fitness family." Have T-shirts made up like the ones I've had made for my family that say TEAM SCHWARZENEGGER.

► Get in the habit, as a family, of going against the labor- and effort-saving American life-style. Mow your lawns together, shovel snow, take out your trash, walk up stairs instead of using escalators, walk to places when you can instead of driving. Make a family *point* of this; it's something else you can be proud of.

► Never force any family member to exercise when he or she doesn't want to. The point is to create a family atmosphere where everyone is naturally and voluntarily physically active. Don't impose any program, including the ones in this book, on anyone, ever. Make each other *want* to do them.

► Give over a room or an area of your house to play, rainy-day exercising, and roughhousing. Set up a Nerf basketball goal, a mini-trampoline; fill the room with skills and exercise toys and games —and then use them.

▶ Create your own annual "Bowl Games" or "World Series." Charles Gaines's family holds an annual Thanksgiving touch-football game for neighborhood kids and adults, and every Fourth of July they put on a "World Series" neighborhood softball game.

▶ Create regular "family fitness days," "fitness weekends," "fitness parties," and "Backyard Olympics." (At the end of this chapter, I'll tell you how to do those things.)

▶ Make your family vacations active ones. Canoe trips, biking adventures, hiking or climbing expeditions, and cross-country ski tours make great family vacations. Or go to a family resort where there is a wide range of sports and exercises and try them all. My friend Dr. Bob Arnot is a fitness-vacation fanatic. On an average day at a resort while he and his family are on vacation, they will play two sets of tennis, windsurf for a couple of hours, take a ten-mile bike ride, waterski for an hour or two, and then cap the day off with a gym workout and a hike. Now *that's* the kind of family fitness enthusiasm I like!

▶ Most of all: keep it imaginative and keep it fun!

a family fitness program for ages six and seven

Three Days Per Week:

Five minutes of warm-up;
fifteen minutes of continuous aerobic exercise, play, or games;
five minutes of cool-down.

Two Days Per Week:

Twenty minutes of skill drills or games.

a family fitness program for ages eight, nine, and ten

Three Days Per Week:

Five minutes of warm-up;
twenty minutes of continuous aerobic exercise;
five minutes of cool-down.

Two Days Per Week:

Fifteen minutes of stretching;
fifteen minutes of strength training;
five minutes of cool-down.

One Day Per Week:

Thirty minutes of skill drills or games.

assembling your program

I have designed both these programs to be actually *created* by you—child and parent together.

Here's what you do. In Appendix A of this book, there is a collection of aerobic exercises and games—some marked "For Ages Six and Seven," some "For Ages Eight, Nine, and Ten," and some marked as appropriate for both age groups. After you have read the section below called "Aerobic Exercise and Games"—which will tell you what you need to know about the role aerobic activities should play in your program—go to the back of the book and choose the exercises and/or games that you want to plug into your program (for fifteen minutes a day, three days a week, for ages six or seven; and for twenty minutes a day, three days a week, for ages eight, nine, or ten).

Do the same for the motor-skills drills and games listed in Appendix B—first read the section below called "Motor Skills," then go to the back of the book and pick the drills and games you want to put into your program (again, some are marked just for ages six and seven, some for ages eight, nine, and ten, and some for both).

For ages eight through ten, there are paragraphs below on flexibility and strength training, and I've included some good stretching exercises in Appendix C, and strength exercises in Appendix D, that you can choose from to fill in those parts of your program. Some of the stretching exercises are also marked as being appropriate for six- and seven-year-olds to use before and after aerobic activity.

Have you ever eaten in a cafeteria? You get a tray and go down the line and pick exactly what foods you want. You might get a salad and I might get a sandwich; you might get chicken and I might get soup. Both of us can pick whatever we like to eat, and we can change what we get every day so we don't get bored always eating the same thing. Well, that's the way I've designed these programs—so that you can choose your own exercises and games, and vary them whenever you want.

Now here are a few things you need to know before you start down the cafeteria line:

▶ It doesn't really matter which days of the week you choose to do your program, but I recommend that you alternate your aerobic workout days with your skills (or skills,

strength, and flexibility) days. For the six- and seven-year-olds, a good schedule would be: aerobics on Mondays, Wednesdays, and Fridays; skills on Tuesdays and Thursdays; and maybe a "Fitness Day" or a "Fitness Party" over the weekend. (These and other special "fitness occasions" are described in Part III of this chapter.) For eight-through ten-year-olds: aerobics on Mondays, Wednesdays, and Fridays; strength and flexibility on Tuesdays and Thursdays; and skills on any day you choose. But remember that *regularity* is the key to staying on an exercise program. Set up your program schedule however is convenient for you, and then *stay with it*.

▶ Though it is all right to plug different exercises and games into your program every day if you want to, I suggest that you stick with a particular kind of aerobic exercise (or a particular game), and a particular set of skill drills and/or games, etc., for at least one week at a time. Often it takes at least that long to get familiar enough with the exercise or game to get the full fitness benefit from it.

▶ It is okay for parents and kids to be doing different exercises during a workout (or for a parent to be doing more helping, encouraging, or coaching than actual exercising). What's critically important—at least until your child is old enough and motivated enough to do his or her program *properly* and *regularly* alone—is that you do the workouts *together*—every day, every week.

▶ Don't assume that because your child is getting some exercise at school and/or through community programs, you don't need a family fitness program, or only need it sometimes (like in the summer). The real point of family fitness activity is to make regular exercise an ingrained, daily, lifelong practice with your child. Schools and community programs can give kids exercise (sometimes enough); *you* can make it a habit.

aerobic exercise and games

As you have already learned in Chapter 1, "aerobic exercise" is exercise that strengthens the heart and lungs and helps them to do more work more efficiently. It is exercise that makes your heart and lungs deliver more oxygen to your body than usual for an extended period of time. For someone running a marathon, that period of time is usually over two hours; for a triathlete it can be for as long as *eight hours*.

For an aerobic exercise session to really do you any good, continuous movement (exercise) has to be kept up for at least fifteen minutes at a brisk level, causing your heart and lungs to work harder than usual, but not too hard.

▶ How do you know when your heart and lungs are working hard enough, but not too hard? You can tell exactly by taking your pulse, but that's difficult to do while you're exercising or playing, so I recommend you use what I call the "talk test." During your aerobic exercises or games you should be exercising hard enough so that you are breathing heavily but not so heavily that you can't talk. You should be able to talk to one another or to yourself (with maybe just a little puffing, but not much) *while* you exercise. If you can't, you are exercising too hard. After a few aerobic workouts, you'll learn to "listen to your body." If it tells you, "This isn't hard enough; I'm not even breathing fast," then step up the exercise a little. If it tells you, "Hey, I'm running out of breath here . . . can't talk . . . I'm too hot!"—then slow down. Pretty soon you'll know just how hard you should be exercising all the time.

▶ When you first start doing the aerobic part of your program, you may find that you can't exercise at all without getting too tired. That's okay. If you find, for example, that you can't run for fifteen minutes straight, run for as long as you can (and still talk), and then walk briskly for the rest of the time. As the running gets easier for you (and it will), run for a longer time and walk less. When you're running slowly for the whole fifteen minutes and *that* gets easy, run faster or run for a longer period of time. Just listen to your body, and it will tell you when you are exercising or playing hard enough, but not too hard.

▶ It is very important that your aerobic exercise or play be done *continuously* (without stopping)—for fifteen minutes in the six- through seven-year-old program and for twenty minutes in the eight- through ten-year-old program. You *can* combine exercises or games by going from one to another during the fifteen or twenty minutes, as long as you don't stop for more than a few seconds between them. For example, you could run for five minutes, then go on to five minutes of calisthenics, followed immediately by five minutes of aerobic tag, for as good a workout as fifteen minutes of any one of those things would give you.

▶ You should always warm up before your aerobic workout and cool down after it. I've recommended five minutes of warm-up and five minutes of cool-down for both programs. Warm up with walking, walking in a circle, calisthenics, jumping jacks, or with some of the stretching exercises in Appendix C. The best way to cool down is to walk slowly for two or three minutes after your exercises or games and then do some simple stretching exercises. The point of warming up is to prepare your muscles and heart for vigorous exercise, and the cool-down is to bring your body back down safely and slowly from hard work to rest. Both are *very important,* so don't try to save a little time by skipping them.

▶ The aerobic games I've listed in the back are a great way to make exercise appealing, particularly for younger kids with short attention spans. But once you've got your program rolling, parents should encourage even young kids to begin mixing some of the "life fitness" aerobic exercises and sports (e.g., walking, running, swimming, cycling, rowing, cross-country skiing, jumping rope) with the games. After a while the exercises should completely replace the games, but only after they are as "fun" for the kid as the games are.

Aerobic exercise, no matter how you get it, is so good for you in so many ways that it is almost like a magic tonic. It not only strengthens your heart and lungs, it also helps burn off fat, gives you more energy, improves your muscle tone, and even helps you to concentrate and think better. It is the single most important form of exercise you can do, all your life, so let your program turn it into a lifetime practice for you.

motor skills

Motor skills are sometimes called "athletic skills," but they are more than that—they are the building blocks of movement that allow us to do everything we do with our bodies.

You have to be *ready* to learn any new motor skills. Being ready means: (1) that you have already learned the skills you need to learn *before* you can go on to the new one; (2) that you are old enough, or mature enough, to learn it; and (3) that you want to learn it.

To accomplish any complicated bodily movement—such as hitting a tennis ball over the net, or ice skating—a number of motor skills have to work together in what we call a "motor program." No one can just walk out onto a tennis court and hit the ball across the net until all of the skills that make up that motor program have been developed up to a certain level. (Some of those skills are balance, eye-hand coordination, dexterity, and visual tracking.)

The best way to learn to hit a tennis ball over a net, or any other motor program in or out of sports, is to *learn each of the necessary skills as well as you can when you are ready to learn it* —in other words, to break the program down into units of skills and to master each of those units, rather than trying to learn the whole program at once. For this reason, kids who begin mastering the basic skills that underly all sports and good movement when they are very young have a huge head start not only on athletic performance but on all fitness activities as well.

The skill drills and games I have included in Appendix B are ones designed to develop many of the skills that are most central to sports and lifetime fitness activities. Among those skills are: kicking, catching, throwing, reaction time, eye-foot coordination, eye-hand coordination, whole-body coordination, balance, balance stabilization, foot speed, visual tracking, and agility. Kids between six and ten should be able to develop and improve all of these skills with the drills and games given here.

Some of the drills and games are labeled for six- and seven-year-olds and others for ages eight, nine, and ten, but if you are six or seven and want to try one of the games or drills for older kids, go right ahead. I'd recommend that you pick one or two of the drills or one of the games for each skills workout and work on them for at least three or four workouts before going on to others. Remember, the point is to *master,* not try out, as many skills as possible.

A *few* kids of eight, nine, and ten may be getting all the skills practice and learning they need in school or community or country-club sports programs. If you are ten years old, go to soccer and hockey camps, play those sports regularly in school, play tennis, waterski all summer, and ski with your parents in the winter, the games and drills here are not likely to benefit you much. But the *great majority* of kids in this age range are *not* getting enough training from schools and community programs. If you or your parents are in any doubt, try the drills and games given in this book. If you can do them all easily and well, you don't need them; if you can't, you do.

Here is a list (adapted from Dr. Kenneth Cooper's *Kid Fitness*) of twenty-one very basic skills and the ages at which most kids learn them. This list is meant only to serve as a guideline for parents—to give you an idea of where your child stands with basic skills development *before* you begin your family program. Again, this list is a general guideline—don't worry if your child hasn't developed a particular skill by the indicated age. You should, however, encourage him or her to master *all* these skills as soon as he or she is ready to learn them.

Skill	Age
Running smoothly	4–5
Jumping, overall skillful execution	5
Galloping, skillfully	6½
Sliding, sideways on two feet as on ice, skillfully	6½
Skipping, skillfully	6½
Throwing, mature overarm pattern (see illustration)	6–8
Catching (trapping ball to chest)	4
Catching, using hands to grasp ball	5
Catching; mature pattern for large balls (see illustration)	6½
Catching, judging flight projections of smaller balls from various distances and angles, as with baseballs, flyballs, and catching punts	10–11

Skill	Age
Kicking rolled ball (as in soccer or kickball)	5–6
Dribbling soccer ball with feet	6–8
Punting (dropping ball and kicking it in the air)	5–6
Dribbling a ball with one hand	5–6
Striking an object sidearm with a stick or racquet	4
Striking an object with stick or bat using two-arm batting motion (NOTE: The ability to strike *moving* objects usually comes between six and eight years.)	4–5
Balancing on one foot for ten seconds	4
Supporting body in basic inverted position, as in rudimentary headstand with feet off floor and knees on elbows	6
Walking on a two- or three-inch beam, using foot-over-foot alternating steps	4½
Hopping on one foot, skillfully	6
Riding a two-wheel bike (without training wheels)	5–6

flexibility

As small children we are all naturally flexible, but as we get older we begin losing joint and muscle flexibility unless we do regular stretching exercises to keep it. Good flexibility in joints and muscles helps prevent injuries such as muscle pulls and bad backs; it also is very important to sports performance and helps us move through life more easily and gracefully.

Very few people, adults or children, enjoy stretching exercises when they first begin doing them, and often those exercises can seem like a waste of time. But if you stick with them, you'll find that they *do* become enjoyable, even addictive, and the loose, warmed-up, relaxed feeling they give your body more than justifies the time it takes to do them.

There are two types of stretches: muscle stretches, for muscle flexibility; and range-of-motion stretches, for joint flexibility. It is important to do both. Range-of-motion stretches carry a joint through part or all of its entire range of motion—like swinging your arm slowly in a 360-degree circle to exercise the range of motion in your shoulders, or rolling your head around for your neck. A muscle stretch simply stretches out a particular muscle and holds it there for a few seconds.

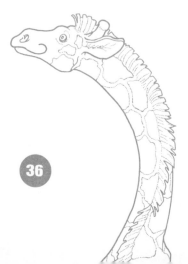

Any time is a good time to stretch (I do stretches while I'm flying in an airplane, while I'm watching TV or a movie, and while I'm working in my office), but it is particularly good to stretch before, and after, doing vigorous exercise—before, in order to warm up the muscles, and after, to keep them from getting stiff. I recommend that all of you do a few stretches before and after your aerobic workouts, and that kids of eight to ten years do fifteen minutes of stretching before strength workouts.

Here are some important tips on *how* to do your stretching exercises:

▶ Start your stretching with range-of-motion, or "limbering up," stretches. This will warm up your muscles for muscle stretching.

▶ The proper way to do a muscle stretch is to stretch out the muscle slowly (no bouncing, ever!) until you feel a mild tug of tension in it. Relax and hold that position for five seconds, then stretch the muscle a little farther until you feel another tug. Now hold that position for as long as the exercise calls for. Breathe slowly and deeply as you stretch and don't hold your breath. Never bounce, and never force a muscle to stretch to the point of pain.

▶ Don't stretch very sore or injured muscles.

▶ Take your time. Don't hurry your stretching, just enjoy it and the nice easy way it makes your body feel when you are finished.

muscular strength and endurance

Over 75 percent of America's girls and almost 30 percent of our boys cannot do a single pull-up! This fact indicates that American boys and girls have much less muscular strength and durance than they need to be physically fit for good health. I'm not saying you need big muscles like mine to be healthy, but strong muscles with good endurance improve our posture, protect us from injury, and help keep us from developing lower-back (and other joint and muscle) problems.

Muscle strength and endurance are also very important to many sports, particularly ones like tennis and swimming, where certain muscle groups have to keep working over a long period of time.

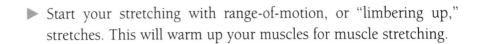

Some people think that strength is a boy thing only, *but it is as important to the good health of girls as it is to boys.* Girls between eight and ten years of age should do the same strength and muscle endurance exercises given in the back of the book as the boys do.

I don't believe boys and girls ten and under should lift weights. The exercises I've given here all use your body's own weight for resistance rather than weights, but if you do them as I recommend, you can get as much benefit from them as you can from exercises with weights.

Here are some tips for how best to do your strength training:

▶ I recommend you do at least one exercise from each of the muscle group divisions I give in the back of the book every time you do your strength workout (that is, one exercise for stomach, one for legs, one for chest, etc.). After a while, you'll probably want to do two exercises per muscle group. Start with one set of as many repetitions as you can comfortably do for each exercise, and as you get stronger, increase the repetitions and go to two and then three sets for each exercise. (A *repetition* is one performance of the exercise—for example, a single sit-up; a *set* is a group of repetitions done without stopping.) You should rest for twenty to thirty seconds between sets.

▶ Never push a muscle to the point where it hurts. Take it easy and increase your reps gradually.

▶ Breathe normally. Don't hold your breath while doing resistance exercises.

▶ Concentrate on each exercise. This is one of the secrets of productive resistance training —*think* about the muscles you are working and concentrate on doing the exercise properly.

▶ Don't expect your muscles to get big from the exercises given here. Increases in muscle size and definition don't happen until puberty. But your muscle strength and endurance *will* improve from the exercises in this book, and that is what is important for your health and for sports performance.

▶ As with all forms of exercise, the key to getting real benefits from strength training is *regularity*. Pick a time—two days a week—when it is convenient for you to do your half hour of stretching and strength exercises, and try to do them at that time *every* week without missing. One advantage these exercises have over weight training is that they are portable—you can do them at camp, at a friend's house, anywhere.

▶ If a particular muscle group gets sore from your training, exercise other muscle groups until the soreness goes away. Don't try to strength-train a sore muscle or muscle group.

▶ If you have a particular body part weaker than the others, spend more time training it.

III. special family fitness events

As I've said before, I want fitness to become a fun, normal, and necessary part of your family's life. Your weekly exercise program should be a pleasurable family routine—as enjoyable and regular as the evening meal. But to help keep exercising fun and fresh for everyone in your family, you should also create and put on special family fitness events as often as possible.

fitness days

Whenever my brother and I had a school holiday while we were growing up in Austria, my father would take the whole family up into the mountains near our home for a "play day." We would fill up the car with soccer balls, jump ropes, kites—or sleds and skis if it was winter—and zoom up the highway into the mountains to a big valley meadow that my uncle owned.

Lots of times we took other kids and adults with us, or met my uncle and his family at the meadow, and we would spend the whole day running and playing games and sports, with the only time out being for a huge, healthful picnic lunch. We would come back just before dark, tired and sunburned and struggling to stay awake to see which kid could count the most cows along the road back home.

You can do your own version of this. Whenever you have a free day, give it over to fun family play and exercise. It doesn't matter whether you go out into the country for your fitness days, or to a city park, or just stay at home. What count are imagination and energy!

Take the family for a hike up a local mountain, or go for a daylong bike ride; rent a couple of canoes and canoe down a river; or put some lunch in a pack and go cross-country skiing for a day. If you live in a city, parks are great places for fitness days. You'd be surprised at how many different games and sports you can pack into a day in the park. Tag, volleyball, touch football, soccer, softball, basketball, roller skating, Frisbee, gymnastics, tennis round-robins, calisthenics, bicycling, street hockey, ice skating—these are all great fitness-day activities that can be done in parks, and there are lots more. I think the best fitness days are when you combine a lot of different activities—doing an hour or so of one thing, then an hour or so of another, all through the day. Just keep it fun for everyone in the family, and keep it active.

fitness weekends

Fitness weekends are really just two fitness days together. Try to set aside at least one weekend a month as a fitness weekend for the whole family. Go hiking, or skiing, or canoeing, or stay at home and put together a two-day schedule of games and sports.

fitness parties

Get your friends involved—adults and kids—with fitness parties. Ultimate Frisbee is a great party game, so is tug-of-war. And a late-afternoon softball game goes great with a barbecue. Let every member of the family throw at least one fitness party a year and choose what you are going to do and whom to invite. One of my family's favorite fitness parties is called the Backyard Olympics.

backyard olympics

You can invite as many as fifteen guests, kids and adults, for a Backyard Olympics. Have a family meeting before the party and decide which events you want to include in your Olympics, and be sure to include events for all ages and sexes. Between six and ten events is a good number for an afternoon party, and you can have up to fifteen or so for an all-day party. Make up scorecards for each event, and when people arrive, have them print their names on the card for each event they want to participate in. Designate one person in your family as the "Official Scorer" (he or she can also participate in the Olympics). Choose events that can be individually measured (that is, in time, distance, accuracy, etc.), and have your scorer explain the rules and scoring of the event to each participant. (In my family, the scorer is free to give out handicaps and disqualify adults who try too hard

whenever he or she wants to.) If you want to, you can make up funny "medals" or prizes to award in each event for first place on through as many places as you'd like. We even put our winners up on a box and sing invented national anthems to them.

Here are a few events you might want to include in your Backyard Olympics, along with the ones you make up yourself.

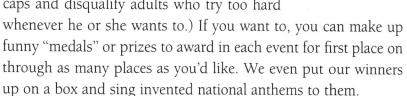

the montreal egg throw: Each Olympian sees how far he or she can throw an uncooked egg on grass without breaking it. Scoring: how many inches or feet the egg is thrown by each competitor.

the seoul bag-hop barrel race: Each Olympian stands in an old feed bag, laundry bag, or pillowcase, holds it up, and hops in it along a course around one or more barrels (or trees). Scoring: how long it takes a competitor to hop from the starting line around the course and back. This event can also be done as a pairs race, with one leg of each of the partners in the bag.

the munich nerf football throw: Hang an old tire from a rope and start it swinging slowly. The Olympian stands as far away from the tire as the scorer decides is fair and tries to throw a Nerf (soft foam) football through the swinging tire. Scoring: number of times the ball goes through the tire out of ten tries.

the barcelona hexagonal jump: See the instructions for the hexagonal jump in Appendix B. Scoring: number of seconds it takes to complete two or three circuits of the hexagonal.

the los angeles obstacle course: We always include this event in our Backyard Olympics, though we change the obstacles frequently. An Olympian starts when the scorer says "Go" and has to get through an obstacle course as fast as possible. The course can be made up however you want. For example, crawl through a section of pipe, do ten sit-ups, climb over a gate, run through tires, roll down a hill, do ten sit-ups, then do two somersaults to the finish line. Scoring: how long it takes a competitor to get through the course, or how funny he or she looks while doing it.

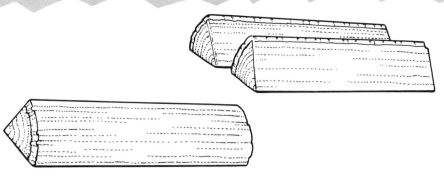

arnold learns the value of hard work at an early age

My father first taught me about the importance of hard work when I was only six years old. He taught me so well that I remember the very day when he gave me my first lesson.

It was a winter day in the little town of Thal, Austria, where I grew up, and my brother and I were in the kitchen playing by the woodbox while our mother cooked lunch. She hummed as she peeled potatoes and onions, and every so often looked down at Meinhard and me, to make certain we were not too close to the wood stove. It was very cold outside, so the stove was filled with logs to keep us warm and snug.

"Be careful of the stove, boys," my mother said. "It is very hot and will burn your skin if you touch it."

Her look was very serious and we knew not to get too close to the stove.

Just then the kitchen door opened wide and a rush of cold air came in and made us shiver. In the doorway stood my father. He was so big that he almost filled the entire frame of the doorway, and we could only see a little of the outside behind him.

"Brrrrr. Close the door, Gustav," my mother said. "We'll lose all our heat."

My father closed the door and looked down at Meinhard and me. His cheeks were red and he was smiling.

"Ah, what a beautiful day. What a glorious day! I don't know if ever I have seen such a day. And don't my fine young sons agree?" my father said.

Meinhard and I laughed and nodded our heads. We were happy because our father was smiling and he didn't seem to mind the pile of splinters we had made by pulling long slivers from a log that belonged in the woodbox.

"Aha!" my mother said as she clapped her hands. "What your father really means, boys, is that today the lake is officially frozen. Today is glorious because your father can practice ice curling."

"You are right!" my father said. "The lake is frozen, so now I can practice for the championships. But this year I will not practice alone. This year I will have assistants to help me clean the ice and retrieve my stones."

"And where did you find such willing assistants?" my mother asked.

"Right . . . here," my father said as he reached down and swept up Meinhard and me in each of his arms and spun us around.

Meinhard and I looked at each other as our father held us in the air. It didn't matter that neither of us knew what "assistants" were or what they did. Our father's joy was wonderful and contagious. We were going to have an exciting day!

"Come now and eat lunch," my mother said. "Then you and your assistants can go practice for the championships."

My father sat and ate, but Meinhard and I were so excited about going to the lake with our father that we didn't want to eat the bowls of goulash my mother had put before us. We wanted to leave right away, without a moment's delay.

"It is important to eat your stew," my mother said. "If you don't eat properly, you can't exercise properly."

When we finished our lunch, Meinhard and I dressed in thick wool pants and sweaters and ran outside to join our father. He was loading a sled with brooms and a shovel and ice-curling equipment. Because our house was close to the lake, we could see people walking out on the ice, and it made Meinhard and me very excited to be on our way. Then my father turned to us and said, "Good. Now we have everything we need. Are my assistants ready?" We nodded eagerly and followed him as he pulled the sled down a snow-covered meadow that bordered the lake.

It was fun walking on the ice. In some areas there was a thin layer of snow that looked like someone had sprinkled sugar or flour over the ice. And in other areas the ice was black and smooth and very slippery, and Meinhard and I could run and slide across the icy surface. When we were almost to the other side of the lake, my father said, "This is a good place to practice. Here the wind has kept the snow from gathering in drifts and the ice is the smoothest on the lake."

My father unpacked the sled and gave Meinhard and me each a small broom. Then he took the shovel and said, "Follow me with your brooms and sweep away what I miss with the shovel. It is very important that you do a good job and make the ice as smooth as possible. The smoother the ice, the farther my curling stone will slide."

Our father pushed his shovel through the thin layer of snow so fast that Meinhard and I had to walk very fast to keep up. We swept away all the pieces of ice and clumps of snow that my father's shovel had skipped over. When we were way down the lake, maybe four hundred feet from where we had started, my father turned around and said, "Now we go back and do the same thing next to the path we just made."

We went up and down the lake following our father until the path was ten feet wide. Sweeping was hard work, but it was also fun, especially when Meinhard and I made a game of sweeping the loose snow and ice into the air.

When my father was satisfied with our work, he turned to Meinhard and me and said, "Good. This is a wonderful alley for me to practice on."

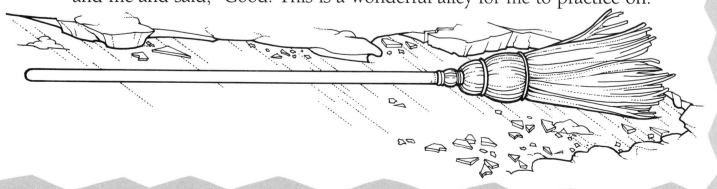

Then he put down his shovel and picked up two curling stones and a long stick that looked like the kind used in shuffleboard. The stones, which were not really stones but pieces of hardwood, weighed fifteen pounds each and had a metal ring around them. The long stick was used to propel the stone down the alley.

"Now, I am going to hurl these stones down the alley as far as I can," my father said. "I want you two to chase after them until they come to a stop. Then there will be a contest to see who can push his stone back to me the fastest."

My father took hold of the wooden handle that sticks up from the top of the stone and began to swing the stone backward and forward. Meinhard and I stood next to the alley and watched our father swing the stone in longer and longer arcs, putting his entire upper body into it like a discus thrower. Then with a big grunt, he released the stone. It flew out over the ice for forty or fifty feet, then landed on its flat bottom and slid wobbling down the alley.

"Go, Meinhard," my father said. "Hurry, or you will never catch it." Meinhard ran after the stone, but he kept falling down on the ice. He didn't catch up to the stone until he was halfway down the alley. My father cheered Meinhard on while I anxiously waited for my turn.

"Are you ready, Arnold?" my father said. I nodded yes and waited for him to release the stone. Down at the far end of the alley Meinhard waved his arms and called out for me to join him. When my father released the stone, I started to run, but immediately slipped and fell to my knees.

"Get up, Arnold," my father said. "Don't give up. You can catch it. Run, run!"

I got up and started running after the stone again. My father and Meinhard cheered me on as I kept running and falling, running and falling. By the time I made it to the end of the alley, the stone had already come to a complete stop. Even though it made me mad to keep falling and not catch up with the stone, it was fun chasing after it and I wanted to do it again.

"Now we push them back," Meinhard said. He bent down and grabbed the handle of the stone between his legs. Then he leaned forward, so that he looked like a sprinter about to take off.

I slid the other stone next to Meinhard's and then copied his stance. I was so excited for the race to begin that I felt as if there were a hundred butterflies in my stomach trying to get out.

"Bet I beat you," Meinhard said.

"Bet you don't," I said.

"Ready, set, GO!" Meinhard yelled. And he was suddenly pushing the stone up the alley between his legs toward our father, who was cheering and waving his arms.

"Run, Meinhard! Run, Arnold, faster, faster!" our father yelled.

By the time I started running after Meinhard, he was so far in front of me that he easily won the race. In fact, he won all the races that day. I did not like losing, especially to my brother, but my father would not let me get discouraged. He kept cheering and urging me to run faster and work harder.

When we were walking home at the end of the day, my father said, "So, you did not win a race today. But you were close many times, which is good. It means you never stopped trying. Now you have to practice very hard, harder than your competition. That's how you win."

All that winter I went out with my father whenever he practiced curling, sometimes without Meinhard, who preferred sledding to being on the lake. The instant we reached the lake, I would take one of the stones from my father's sled and start pushing it as fast as I could to the practice area. As a result, my legs and back and arms became very strong. And eventually I did beat Meinhard. In fact, by the end of the next winter, he never beat me again.

My father was right about the importance of hard work. If you want to win, you have to practice harder than your competition. And he was very wise to teach me these lessons at a young age and in a way that made them fun and exciting.

Nutrition

3 eating smart

Of the ten leading causes of death in America, five—atherosclerosis, stroke, heart disease, diabetes, and cancer—can be caused by bad diet. High blood pressure, obesity, and osteoporosis can also be caused by what and how much you eat. Eating dumb, in short, can make us sick, and even kill us. It also robs us of energy, makes our bodies soft and fat, and keeps us from performing well at sports, at school, and on the job. If exercise is half the secret to a long, healthy, fit, and vigorous life, the other half is good nutrition—or what I call "eating smart."

And this is every bit as true for kids as it is for adults. In this chapter, I'll tell you how to get the whole family eating smart. You'll notice I said *the whole family*. Just as parent participation is crucial to getting kids to exercise, parents *have* to eat smart themselves if they want their kids to do so. It just won't work to tell little Suzy to lay off the Twinkies if she sees you sneaking them every chance you get.

Life fitness, as we have seen, is all about developing good habits at an early age. As parents we, of course, do ourselves a huge favor by eating smart, but more important, we are giving our kids perhaps the most valuable gift we can ever give them—a daily example that will encourage them to reap the lifelong, healthful harvest of good nutrition.

Eating smart doesn't mean all sprouts and tofu. Good eating can and should be delicious eating, and once you get used to it, you'll feel sorry for those poor slobs at the take-out window of fast-food places. Good nutrition is not about fads either. Where I grew up no one had ever heard of grapefruit diets or vitamin supplements or fish oil—we just ate good home-cooked country food and grew up healthy and strong on it, the same way our parents and grandparents had. Eating smart is first of all knowing what is good for you and what is not; then it is the simple discipline of practicing that knowledge in the form of good eating habits until those habits become second nature. At the end of this chapter, I'll give you a list of good basic eating habits that you can begin to practice in your family that will get your kids off to the right nutritional start.

One twelve-ounce cola contains nine teaspoons of sugar.

One fast-food hamburger with cheese contains nine teaspoons of solid fat.

But first let's look at what smart eating means for kids ages six through ten. Did you know that over 30 percent of American kids have abnormally high cholesterol levels? That 99 percent of American kids eat sweet desserts at least six times a week? And that, on average, American kids drink twenty-four ounces of soda pop a day? Basically, what's wrong with the diet of American kids (and it is drastically and dangerously wrong) is the same thing that's wrong with the diet of American adults: we *all* eat too much sugar and salt (much of them coming from soft drinks, snacks, and fast foods), too much cholesterol and saturated fat (from fast foods, again, lunch meats, fatty red meats, butter, cream, desserts, etc.), and we *don't* eat enough of the bran cereals, whole-grain foods, pastas, rice, beans and peas, fresh vegetables and fruits that supply us with fiber and complex carbohydrates.

You might be thinking, "Okay, Arnold, I've heard all this before, but how do I actually put smart eating into practice in my kid's life?"

Well, the best place to start is with:

breakfast

This is, by far, the most important meal of the day, especially for children, and it should *never* be skipped or skimped. Studies have proven that people who eat breakfast are more productive and alert, tend to study better and perform better at sports, than people who do not. A *good* breakfast provides kids with high-test fuel to run on for the whole day; a bad breakfast (a lot of sugar and/or fat) is the same as putting sugar in their gas tanks.

Eating smart at breakfast for a six- to ten-year-old means getting Vitamin C, calcium, potassium, iron, fiber, and complex carbohydrates. A breakfast that would provide all of that is simple: a bowl of unsugared or *lightly* sugared cereal or oatmeal with low-fat milk and some sliced fruit on top; a glass of orange or grapefruit juice; and a piece of whole-grain toast or an English muffin topped with All Fruit preserves. Waffles and whole-grain pancakes topped with fruit instead of syrup are good too, and eggs are fine two to three times a week (unless there is a history of high cholesterol in your family). Make bacon and sausage a once-in-a-while treat, and skip altogether doughnuts, Danish pastries, Pop Tarts, and anything else that is full of sugar.

lunch

Lunch should be a refill for kids, but again, only with high-test fuel. If you have any question about the quality of the school lunches your children are getting (the lunches at many schools are too high in fat, cholesterol, sugar and salt, and those at many

other schools are so tasteless that kids won't eat them), send them off with a lunch bag or pail two or three times a week. Good high-test lunch foods are fruit, peanut butter (only the nonhydrogenated kind), whole-grain breads, pasta dishes, raw vegetables, nonfat or low-fat yogurt, unsalted nuts, low-sodium soups, and low-fat cheeses. Avoid lunch meats, most of which are way high in fats, and make lunches (or dinners, for that matter) at fast-food restaurants a no more than thrice-a-week treat. (A typical fast-food meal is about 40 percent fat and 20–30 percent sugar, with virtually no fiber and much too much cholesterol and salt —two or three times a week of that is enough!)

dinner

Try to have your evening meal together, as often as you can, as a family—it gives you not only a chance to share the day with one another but an opportunity to turn smart eating into an enjoyable ceremony. Turn off the TV, put away the paper, take the phone off the hook, sit around a table (I know you're busy; who isn't? *Make* the time), and *enjoy* a good, well-prepared, nutritious meal together. That's what family dinners are all about, and those kinds of meals not only top off your child's nutrition for the day, they teach kids that eating is something to be taken seriously, and to be done with care and style.

Dinners don't have to be huge—in fact, it's better for you if they are not. Make sure they include some good protein (fish, poultry, or lean meats, or beans or peas); some complex carbohydrates (a baked potato, pasta, rice, or steamed vegetables); a little whole-grain bread; and maybe some fruit for dessert. Learn how to cook without fats, to prepare good, low-fat, low-salt salad dressings, to steam vegetables, to make your own nutritious breads and pastas. There are lots of healthful-eating cookbooks around, and this kind of cooking and eating is *fun,* as well as delicious and good for you. The more attention you pay to how and what you eat in the family, particularly at dinnertime when you are all together, the more likely it is your child will develop smart eating as a lifetime habit.

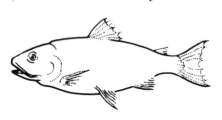

snacks

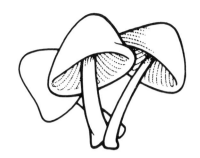

There is nothing wrong with snacks for kids six to ten, as long as they are the right kind. Candy bars, jelly doughnuts, potato chips, cookies, and cupcakes are not the right kinds of snacks, and can actually *rob* your kid of energy. Raw vegetables, fresh fruits, unsalted nuts, nonfat or low-fat yogurt, oatmeal cookies, bran muffins, raisins, cereal, fruit juice, gorp or trail mix—these are all the *right* kinds of snacks, and kids can get as used to them (and fond of them) as they can of the wrong kinds.

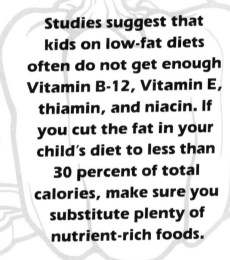

Studies suggest that kids on low-fat diets often do not get enough Vitamin B-12, Vitamin E, thiamin, and niacin. If you cut the fat in your child's diet to less than 30 percent of total calories, make sure you substitute plenty of nutrient-rich foods.

a note about obesity

Millions of children in this country suffer from the disease of obesity (defined as being 20 percent heavier than one should be for one's height, according to the life insurance height/weight tables). It is a very serious disease that can lead to high blood pressure, heart disease, diabetes, and some forms of cancer. In addition, obese children are in danger of serious, life-crippling emotional and psychological damage.

If you suspect your child may be obese, find out. You can do that by taking him or her to a doctor, or by having administered a skinfold caliper test that will determine the child's body-fat percentage. The key to losing weight safely and permanently is to do it *gradually* through a combination of sensible diet and exercise. If your child is simply a little overweight, you and he can easily correct that with an exercise program and smart eating, as described here. If you learn that your child is obese, I strongly recommend that you seek medical help.

smart eating habits your family should develop

Now here are some good basic eating habits—some of them taken or adapted from Dr. Kenneth Cooper's "Positive Eating Plan"—that you and your family should try to develop. You'll be surprised at how easy it is to incorporate these habits into your family life.

▶ Establish consistent eating patterns, including three meals a day.

▶ Eat a balanced diet, with a variety of foods at each meal, to include 50 percent carbohydrates, 20 percent protein, and 30 percent fat.

▶ Don't eat more than you need—push away from the table *before* you are full.

▶ Prepare foods in ways that minimize the use of fat (that is, steaming vegetables instead of frying them in butter or lard; broiling or grilling chicken rather than frying it; using Pam when you do fry).

▶ Eat only low-calorie, low-salt snacks.

▶ Drink six to eight glasses of liquid, preferably water, daily.

▶ Eat slowly, chew your food well, and only *eat* while you're eating—no TV or reading. Also, try to eat every meal sitting at a table, not while standing, walking around, or driving.

▶ Get your kids to help with the meal planning, shopping, cooking, table setting, and cleaning up. *Discuss* food with them—what's good for them and what's not and why.

▶ Don't keep food in the house that you don't want your kids to eat. Do keep plenty of the foods you *want* them to eat and make them easily available, such as fruit in a basket.

▶ Encourage your kids to carry a "health lunch" to school at least twice a week.

▶ Come to a family agreement on how often you will eat "fast foods" (it should be no more than two or three times a week), and *all* of you stick to it. And when you do eat at fast-food places, go for a chicken sandwich instead of a cheeseburger, or best of all, try the salad bar.

▶ Try to eat dinner together as a family at least five nights a week.

▶ If you have to skip a meal, never let it be breakfast.

▶ Help your child acquire tastes for new foods that are healthful and nutritious, such as asparagus, oysters, yams, watercress. The wider your child's taste in foods, the easier and more fun smart eating becomes. But also remember you will never help a child to like a particular food by forcing him to eat it.

▶ There are plenty of good books on how and why to eat smart. Get one or two and read them.

▶ Eating, like exercise, is one of the great pleasures in life. Do it smart, but *enjoy it*, and teach your children to enjoy it.

annaliese teaches arnold a lesson about skills

When I was eight years old, our nearest neighbors were the Volroyds. Their son, Sigmund, was my best friend. Sigmund and I wanted to be on our school soccer team, and during the two-mile walk to the schoolhouse every morning we would practice kicking a soccer ball back and forth between us. Our legs were strong from playing in the fields that summer and we could kick the ball a very long way. Even though I couldn't kick it as far as Sigmund or my brother, I could still kick it a long distance. We both imagined we would be the strongest kickers in our school, and looked forward to all the goals we would score when the soccer season began.

One day in the fall, a new family moved into the farm next to the Volroyds. They had a daughter named Annaliese, who was the same age as Sigmund and I were. At times she would walk to school with us, but Annaliese didn't talk much, so we paid little attention to her. We would just go on kicking our soccer ball as far as we could between us.

One morning Annaliese said in a quiet voice, "You boys don't know how to dribble. It doesn't matter how far you can kick the ball if you can't dribble." Sigmund and I stood and stared at her.

"Give me the ball, Arnold," said Annaliese, "and then both of you try to take it back."

Annaliese put the ball on the ground and began passing it between her feet. She was as quick as a trout, and she ran all around and between us, the ball flying back and forth between her black shoes. Sigmund and I couldn't get it away from her no matter how hard we tried. Once she even kicked the ball between my legs and picked it up again behind me! That made me try even harder to kick the ball away from her, but no matter how hard I tried, I couldn't do it. I realized that our attempts to get the ball back were hopeless; in fact, the situation now seemed so funny that I began laughing. I laughed so hard that I had to lie down on the grass. Sigmund started laughing too, and he fell down beside me with his tongue hanging out.

Annaliese, who wasn't even breathing hard, flipped the ball into the air with her toe and bounced it off one of her skinny knees four or five times. Then she grinned for the first time since Sigmund and I had met her. I thought it was a nice smile, though I didn't say so to Sigmund.

"Two of my brothers were on the national team," said Annaliese, "and they taught me all about soccer and how to kick and dribble and pass and trap the ball. I can teach both of you, if you want."

Sigmund and I looked at each other and didn't know what to say. It had never occurred to us that a girl could teach boys how to be better soccer players.

"Sigmund and I would be more than happy to have you give us some pointers," I said. And thanks to Annaliese, we really did improve our soccer game and became well-rounded players.

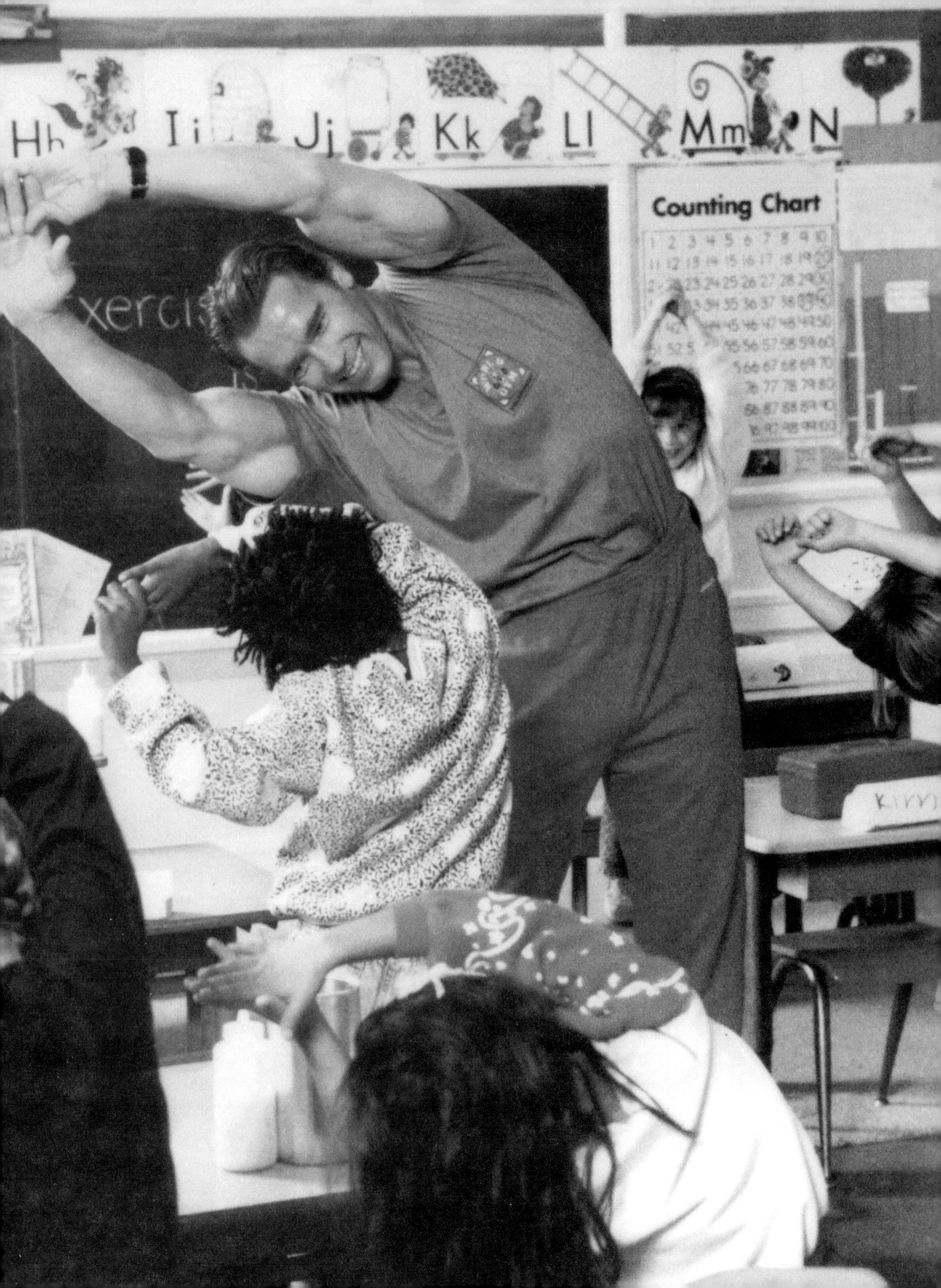
Hh Ii Jj Kk Ll Mm N
Counting Chart

SCHOOL

4 fitness at school

Fitness for children begins, as we have seen, in the home. But it doesn't end there, and neither does your responsibility as a parent to ensure that your child's fitness and health needs are being met.

In my position as chairman of the President's Council of Physical Fitness and Sports, I have visited dozens of elementary schools all over America and have had a firsthand look at their physical education programs. The good news is that some of those school programs are excellent; the bad news is that the great majority of them are not.

One of the strange things I've learned is that many parents don't *know* if the physical education program in their child's school is any good or not, whether or not the child is receiving any health education, or if the child's school lunch program is a healthful, nutritious one. No doubt some parents don't care. But many, many more simply *assume* that the physical activity and nutritional needs of their children are being met by the schools.

More often than not, those parents are wrong. I have talked with many parents, for example, who assume their kids are getting daily physical education. The fact is that nowadays barely one third of American kids in grades one through four are taught physical education daily, and only *one* state in the country, Illinois, requires daily physical education for its students.

The bottom line is that you owe it to yourself and your child to *know exactly* what his or her school is doing with physical education, health education, and nutrition, and in this chapter I will tell you exactly how you can evaluate those things.

If you learn that your child's school is *not* doing a good job in those areas, you very well might decide to encourage the school to improve, and I will give you some suggestions on how best to do that.

And finally, at the end of this chapter I list and briefly describe a few organizations and programs that are specifically dedicated to helping schools and teachers develop or improve the physical fitness component of their physical education instruction.

is your child's school doing a good job?

To evaluate how well, or poorly, a school is contributing to your child's fitness and health, you should visit the school, have a look at the gym and other physical education facilities, have a lunch in the lunchroom, and then sit down with your child's physical education teacher and ask him or her the following questions:

▶ How many times a week does your child participate in physical education classes and how long are those classes? (They should be a minimum of thirty minutes long. Five classes per week is good, three per week is fair, and fewer than three classes a week is poor.)

▶ Are there enough facilities and equipment for every student in every class?

▶ How many students are in each physical education class? (There shouldn't be more than fifteen to twenty kids per instructor.)

▶ Do qualified physical education teachers teach the classes?

▶ Are the physical education opportunities equal for boys and girls? Does the school provide good PE opportunities for disabled kids, kids with chronic diseases like asthma, obese kids, and kids who are unskilled at sports?

▶ Do the physical education classes work on motor skills with first- and second-graders? Do they provide your child with at least fifteen minutes of aerobic exercises three days a week? Do they include stretching and muscular strength and endurance exercises for third- and fourth-graders?

▶ Does the school provide for instruction in the "lifetime fitness activities" (that is, running, swimming, and walking)?

▶ Are team sports at the school relaxed and fun-oriented? Can kids who are not good athletes play on these teams?

▶ Are all kids in the school tested at least twice a year for the key health-related fitness components? Are parents informed of the test results?

► Is your child receiving classroom health education on exercise, nutrition, drug and alcohol abuse, weight control, and so forth?

► Does the school have a healthful, nutritious lunch program? What is it exactly?

making waves

If the answer to the first question above is that classes of at least thirty minutes in length are held three to five days a week, and the other answers are all "yes," your child is one of the lucky few in America who is getting from his school first-rate physical education, supplemental health education, and a good lunch program. If you get *any* "no" answers, the school is not doing everything it should to meet the fitness needs of its students. Once you know that, you can decide what, if anything, you want to do about it. You can either work to improve the physical education and/or lunch programs at your school, move your child to another school, or just let it go and rely on your family fitness program to make up for the school's deficiencies.

If you are at all like me, you will probably want to make a few waves at the school. Here's how to do that with the best chance of success.

First of all, determine exactly and specifically what it is you want to accomplish. It is much more effective to go to a principal or superintendent with concrete suggestions (for example, "We need more exercise mats"; "We need fitness testing twice a year") than with a general complaint.

Second, get your child's physical education instructor and the school's PE director, if there is one, on your side at the very beginning. Most educators want a good program as much as you do and are natural allies in seeking improvement.

Third, understand the financial situation of your school's PE department. How much money does it have? How does it get its funding? Can it get more and, if so, how? Most schools whose physical education programs are not up to snuff will blame it on a lack of funds. Sometimes that's the real reason, sometimes it's not. If money is not the issue, you should find out what the problem really is. And if the lack of money is the main issue, you should try to come up with some workable and creative solutions to overcome the problem.

Fourth, get other parents behind you early on—speak to anyone else who you think will share your concerns, and put together your own lobbying group.

Fifth, understand the chain of command in your child's school and school system and how to negotiate it within that system to achieve your goals.

After you've done all this, you're ready to make your move. If your child's physical education instructor would prefer to work within the system for changes, let the teacher try it. But if he or she doesn't take the initiative, or takes it and fails, go with a number of other parents to see the school principal, to whom you present either a written or verbal petition for change. If your principal can't or won't act, go to see the school district's superintendent. And if that doesn't work, go to the school board with the parents' committee petition.

And if *that* doesn't work (it probably will, if you approach the board properly and have the finances figured out), tell the whole scroungy lot that you're calling in The Terminator!

some quotes from a pro

Sharon Nicosia is the physical education teacher for over five hundred kids, grades one through six, at the Beaver Meadow Elementary School in Concord, New Hampshire, and chairperson of all elementary school physical education programs in the city of Concord. She is an energetic, imaginative, and dedicated educator who has managed to create an excellent program in a school and school district that offer PE only once a week. I asked Sharon to give me a few of her secrets so that I could pass them along here to parents and other physical education teachers. Here is some of what she had to say.

how parents can complement the school physical education program

"Parents and physical education teachers both have a role in fostering a child's health and physical fitness. Find out what your child's physical education program offers him or her. Go and observe your child's program in action or go to a PTA meeting and talk with the physical education teachers there.

"Many skills and activities that are taught in PE can be reinforced at home. If you take the time to find out how your child is doing in PE, it will show your child that PE is just as important as her other subjects in school.

"Many elementary physical education programs take place only once a week. Research has shown us that in order to achieve any improvement in fitness, a person must exercise a minimum of three times per week. Your child's PE program will not meet this need without your involvement in promoting physical activity outside of school. Students who have parent support in improving individual fitness goals can make tremendous gains in personal fitness.

"Take some time each week to exercise as a family, whether it be a bike ride, hike, walk, or even just a softball catch."

what makes great physical education classes for young kids

"*Fun* is the key word. I can't teach a physical education class full of first-graders and not make it fun. They will lose interest. Every day they come through that door they want to know: "What are we doing today? What kind of fun are we going to have?" You can hide the work of becoming physically fit by making it fun.

"Movement experiences must be age appropriate, challenging each child to move and learn at his/her own ability level. Tapping into children's imagination and sense of adventure when planning movement experiences will capture their attention. It could be as simple as walking on their hands and feet, imagining that they are animals moving through the jungle. Add some music that has animal sounds in it and they are off on their first safari. Challenge them to perform certain movement concepts such as light/heavy, fast/slow, low/high, etc. This activity is great for developing upper-body strength and endurance.

"Don't overlook opportunities to integrate other subject areas into their movement experiences. When children move, they can be counting the number of

repetitions children move, they can be counting the number of repetitions of a skill, or spelling various words as they bounce a ball. The spatial concepts such as over, under, through, around, above, can be taught as they are moving.

"Music is a real motivator for children. If you want to set up fitness stations for young kids, so they can do some of the traditional exercises like sit-ups and push-ups, put in a little music and make it a short layout, where they move quickly from one exercise to another. This way, they will think it's fun. Variety is very important, especially for children under eight. If you have them do one thing for too long, they will become bored. You need to keep things short and sweet."

a fabulous multistation exercise program i saw sharon use at her school

"The number of stations you set up will depend on the amount of space and number of students you have in each class. Each station should emphasize one of the five parts of physical fitness: cardiovascular endurance, body composition, muscular strength, muscular endurance, and flexibility. Each exercise station is a great way to teach students which muscle group they are using and what type of fitness they are working on. For instance, one station might be the jump-rope station, where the kids jump rope for one minute to pretaped music. When the music stops, the kids put the equipment down, move to the next station, and start exercising there when the music starts again, and so on.

"Other stations might be for sit-ups, jogging, and dips. I pile up exercise mats for the step aerobics station. And for one station I take a tug-of-war rope and tie it to a pole and stretch it out over the floor. The kids sit on the floor and pull themselves hand-over-hand

to the pole and then run back—that's a great upper-body exercise. There are two or three kids at each station at a time and they change whenever the music stops; the good thing is it frees the teacher up to move from station to station to encourage the kids, to tell them how wonderful and hardworking they are, and to show them proper technique. You can also have them do wrist curls, squeeze a ball, and lift bleach bottles you have filled with sand. You'd be amazed at what you can come up with for stations if you just use your imagination."

teaching kids aerobic exercise

"*Fast* is not the key to aerobic fitness. What works best is to go *slow* and *easy* all the way through the activity for a long period of time. Six- through eight-year-olds have a hard time with that. They don't know the meaning of the word *slow*. With any activity you do with your children, you must try to make them understand that *slow* and *steady* really wins the race to aerobic fitness. And that is a very difficult thing to teach young kids."

the importance of exercise outside of school

"In any given class you're going to have some kids who will peter out in two minutes and you're going to have kids who can go the whole thirty minutes. It all depends on what they do outside of the school environment, how active they are before school, during recess, and after school. If the child is active in some type of aerobic activity or some kind of family fitness program, that child will have a higher level of fitness and motor-skill development."

supplemental school fitness programs

Within the past ten to fifteen years, a number of organizations—including the one I chair, the President's Council for Physical Fitness and Sports—have developed excellent fitness programs for kids that teachers and schools can use to supplement their own physical education curricula. These programs are all directed toward health-related physical fitness (some include nutrition and health education components as well as exercise), and can be particularly valuable to schools whose PE programs are largely or entirely sports-oriented.

I am listing and describing three of these supplemental programs here so that you, as a parent can, if need be, let your child's school and/or physical education teacher know that such programs exist, and also for any teacher who might be reading this book and who feels the need for a little help in his or her fitness instruction.

The President's Council on Physical Fitness and Sports, 701 Pennsylvania Avenue, NW, Washington, DC 20004, telephone (202) 272-3421. The Council provides a fitness test, called the "President's Challenge," for children from ages six through seventeen. School officials can send for a free manual that explains how to administer the test, and for certificates signed by the President to be given to students who qualify for the President's Physical Fitness Award. Children can write the Council requesting its free booklet called *Get Fit,* which suggests exercises for developing strength, flexibility, and endurance.

The President's Youth Fitness Program. A cooperative effort of AAHPERD and the President's Council on Physical Fitness and Sports, this new program is modeled on AAHPERD's Physical Best and the President's Council's President's Challenge. For more information, please contact AAHPERD or the President's Council on Physical Fitness and Sports.

American Alliance of Health, Physical Education, Recreation and Dance (AAHPERD), 1900 Association Drive, Reston, VA 22091, telephone (703) 476-3400. AAHPERD's "Physical Best" program is a comprehensive physical fitness education and assessment program designed to motivate all children and youth to participate in physical activity to develop their *personal best*. Physical Best can help teachers and parents change the way children think about their own physical fitness. This program is the first to combine assessment of health-related fitness with practical classroom instructional materials that teach why and how to stay fit for a lifetime. (Grades K through 12.)

arnold starts a business

Although it wasn't until my early teens that I knew exactly what I wanted to be when I grew up, I already knew at the age of ten that *one* of the things I wanted was to own a business. I didn't know what kind of business, only that I wanted to be my own boss and not someone else's employee. When I told my friends, though, they laughed and said it was impossible for me to know what I wanted at such a young age. But when I told my parents and Mr. Bochman, my elementary school teacher, I was encouraged by them.

"Good, Arnold," they said. "But in order to own a successful business, you have to study very hard." They said I would have to do well in all my subjects, especially mathematics.

"If you don't understand math," Mr. Bochman said, "you will not understand how to be a good businessman. Without an understanding of mathematics, you will not know if you are being paid the right amount or if you are charging the right amount. You won't know if someone is trying to cheat you."

When I realized I could never be a successful businessman if I did not do well in my studies, especially mathematics, I made an extra effort in school. I studied harder and paid closer attention to my teachers. I also learned not to be embarrassed to ask a teacher, or anyone else, for help if I didn't understand a lesson.

Then, in the spring before I started going to the junior high school in the nearby town of Graz, I got my first real job. And by the time school let out for the summer, I had my very first business. I learned firsthand that my parents and teacher had given me sound advice about how important my studies were to being successful in business. I also realized my friends were wrong about my not being able to know what I wanted just because I was a kid.

One morning when I went next door to the Volroyds' farm to get my family's milk, Sigmund met me at the barn and said his father wanted to talk with me.

"Arnold," Mr. Volroyd said, "I need another man to help with the mowing this spring and summer. I know you are good with a scythe, and I can use your help before and after school and on weekends. I will pay you twenty-five cents an hour and lend you a scythe and whetstone. But you must understand that it will not be like helping Sigmund with his chores. You cannot leave and go off and play whenever you want. You must be on time and work hard."

I was very excited and raced home to ask my parents for permission. They said I could work for Mr. Volroyd as long as it didn't interfere with my studies or chores around the house. That night I dreamed about what I would do with the money I would earn. I would work and save until I had enough money to buy a new bicycle. After that I would save to buy something pretty for my mother. Then I would save up so I could go to college and one day have my own business.

I started working for Mr. Volroyd in May, when the first crop of hay was green and juicy and ready to be cut. I woke at four A.M. and met Mr. Volroyd, Sigmund and his older brother Franz, and one other man at the barn. We mowed in the morning because the grass was wet with dew and easier to cut than in the heat of afternoon.

I was given a scythe and a whetstone for keeping the edge of the blade very sharp. A scythe is a long piece of curved wood with two wooden grips for handles and a long crescent-shaped steel blade at the end that is used for cutting hay and grains and weeds. Sigmund, Franz, and I were given a small field of our own to mow. Mr. Volroyd said we could mow

half the field before school and then mow the other half after school let out in the afternoon.

"Make certain you cut the grass low and evenly, boys," Mr. Volroyd said, "or the best part of the crop will be lost." He told us this because the bottom part of the grass is fatter and contains more protein than the top.

The lower the hay is cut, the more nourishment the animals receive when they eat it.

At first we had to concentrate on using the scythe the right way and we did not make good progress. The proper way to use a scythe is to point your feet straight ahead, with your hands squeezing the grips and swinging the scythe backward. Then, when the muscles and tendons are stretched and twisted, the scythe is drawn forward through the hay in a motion that first untwists and then retwists the entire body from right to left. At the end of a swing, the left elbow almost touches the backbone. The blade cuts a five-foot swath of hay that is shaped like a crescent moon.

After a while Franz and Sigmund and I developed a rhythm and we no longer thought about each individual movement with the scythe. All we thought of was the sound of the blade as it swished through the hay and the wonderful smell of freshly cut grass. Even after we would stop every fifteen minutes or so to sharpen our blades with a whetstone, we would fall back into a rhythm. Our bodies meshed perfectly with the scythes and we mowed the hay three rows wide in a clockwise direction around the field. When we were done for the morning, we felt wonderful. The hard work had exercised our muscles and relaxed our minds, and we had accomplished something as well.

I worked for Mr. Volroyd until all his spring hay had been cut and dried and stored in the barn. When we were done, he said I could work for him again in August, when the second crop of hay was ready to be mowed. Though I had earned almost eight hundred schillings (about forty dollars), it was not enough to buy a bicycle—not a good one, anyway—and I thought I would have to wait until after the summer mowing to buy one.

But one day my father came home from work and said he had been telling people in the village about how I was already working and saving money. Several people told him they would hire me to cut weeds around their gardens and fences. I said of course I would cut their weeds. Only I didn't own a scythe or a whetstone.

"Go talk to Mr. Volroyd," my father said. "Maybe he will sell you the scythe you use when you mow for him." And that is exactly what I did.

Mr. Volroyd agreed to sell me the scythe and whetstone for two hundred schillings (about ten dollars), which I paid him from the money I had earned. When I gave him the money, he said, "So, you are going into business for yourself. Remember always to work hard and honestly and to count your money when you are paid."

Within weeks of school being over for the summer, I was working for many people in the village. It seemed everyone in Thal had some small job for me to do. I would be mowing or raking in someone's yard and neighbors would see me and ask if I was interested in doing yard work for them. Of course I was interested! I even cleaned windows and swept sidewalks and steps. I had so much work that I asked my brother, Meinhard, to help me. Although he wanted to be at the lake more than he wanted to work, he agreed to help me because I told him he could not ride my new bicycle when I got it.

"You will have to work and earn money to buy your own bicycle," I said. The thought of his younger brother with a new bicycle while he had none made him so mad that he worked with me the rest of the summer and went to the lake only on weekends.

By the time I went to help Mr. Volroyd mow his summer hay, I had saved seventy-five dollars, which was a fortune and more than enough to buy the bicycle I wanted. And when I added to it the money I earned mowing the summer hay, I could have bought three bicycles. But I didn't. I bought the bicycle I wanted and a pretty silk scarf for my mother. I put the rest of my money in the bank.

When the following summer arrived, I expanded my business to nearby villages. I hired a few of my friends, the same ones who had laughed at me when I first said I wanted to own a business, to work for me as mowers and weeders. And when I told them a few years later that one day I would be a champion bodybuilder and a famous actor as well as a businessman, they did not laugh. They knew that once I made up my mind to do something, I would work hard until I reached my goal.

PROGRAMS

5 community programs, camps, and organized team sports

After home and school, your community is
the third most significant resource of fitness
opportunities and learning for your child.
While it is true that a cutback in funds has
caused there to be fewer community sports
programs in many areas of the country
than there were fifteen or twenty years
ago, it is also true that there are still
plenty of programs remaining in
most communities, *and*

that those programs are, on the whole, better coached, better managed, and more fitness-oriented than ever.

If you have a YMCA in or near your community, you probably have, just in that one resource, more than enough quality sports, aquatic, and fitness programming to keep your entire family busy year round. A typical small-city YMCA that I checked with offers the following sports and fitness programs for kids ages six through ten: Father and Son Sports Time (a different sport each week); Mother and Daughter Sports Time; PeeWee Soccer; PeeWee Basketball; Skipping to Beat (a jump-rope class); Floor Hockey; Tumbling and Gymnastics; a fitness class called "I'm a Fit Kid"; and Swim Team. Other popular Y programs for kids are T-ball, volleyball, aquatics, and walking and running clubs. The YMCA in America presently serves over six million kids annually at 2,072 locations around the country. It is one of the largest providers of before- and after-school child care in the country, and it has recently developed its own youth fitness test and fitness program. According to Lynne Vaughan, the associate director for health and fitness for the U.S. YMCA, the focus of most Y programs is on introducing kids to "the fun of sports and fitness," and virtually all Y's put a strong emphasis on programs that involve various members of the family together.

Another often good and common provider of community youth sports programs is your town or city Recreation and Parks Department. These departments typically offer inexpensive, volunteer-coached programs in youth soccer, basketball, T-ball, track and field, tennis, etc., some of which are usually open to children as young as age six. To find out what programs are available in your community, call the Recreation and Parks Department (sometimes listed as Parks and Recreation) in your town or city (or the nearest town or city to you), or call your state Recreation Department.

Other youth-sports-sponsoring organizations found in many communities are the YWCA, Little League, T-ball leagues, Pop Warner Football, youth hockey leagues, the Boys and Girls Clubs of America, and the Hershey Track and Field Program, which is sponsored nationally by the Hershey Foods Corporation.

You should, of course, personally check out any community-based sports, recreation, or fitness program before committing your child to it. Talk to the program director or coach and make sure that the program or class offers what your child wants to get from it (for example, Little League baseball is likely to be a more competitive sports experience than a town Recreation and Parks Department program). Use the guidelines given below on organized sports to help you ask the right questions and make the right decisions.

And finally, if you can't find in your area exactly the kind of community sports or fitness program you and your child are looking for, and if you have a little extra time and energy, you can always start your own. That's what Bob Glover did. Bob is coauthor of the excellent, comprehensive *Family Fitness Handbook.* In that book he describes how he and his first-grader, Christopher, started an imaginative "success oriented" sports club for Christopher and a bunch of his classmates. Mixing fitness activities with a modified version of baseball and then basketball, Bob and some other volunteer parents created a program for their kids that was healthy, ego-building, and, best of all, so much fun for everyone that Christopher came to prefer it to his birthday and Christmas together. *That's* what you want out of a community youth sports program.

camps

Summer day camps and resident camps can be another good fitness or sports-learning center for your child. There are thousands of resident camps in the United States, with programs ranging from one week to two months, and your first step in picking one out should be to know exactly what your child wants from it. There are weight-loss camps, fitness camps, multisport camps, camps that specialize in a single sport, aquatic camps, outdoor-skills camps, etc., etc. Decide with your child what he or she most wants to accomplish at camp (some examples: to get better at tennis; to learn to canoe; to camp out; to lose weight) before setting out to choose one. Once you have a few camps in mind, call them and request the names and phone numbers of several references.

The YMCA has 409 resident camps around the country with affordable one- and two-week general sports and recreation programs, some of which are open to families. (To learn more about these camps, you can call the YMCA national office in Chicago, toll-free, at (800) 872-9622.) And many town and city recreation and parks departments offer weeklong sports camps in soccer, baseball, basketball, etc., some of them open to kids as young as age six.

Eighty-one percent of the YMCAs in the country offer day camps during the summer—daylong, well-supervised programs in exercise and/or sports—as do many Recreation and Parks Departments, Boys and Girls Clubs, Boy and Girl Scouts, and other community organizations. It is often a good idea to start your child off at one of these day camps before sending him or her off to a resident camp.

Some final words of advice about camps, both day and resident: be as certain as you can that your children will have *fun* at whatever camp you choose; and be *absolutely* certain that they are going because they want to go, and not because you want it for them.

organized team sports

Few experiences in a child's life *can* be as rewarding, as much fun, as educational, and as character-building as participation in team sports. At their best, sports teach cooperation, discipline, self-control, timing, how to set and realize goals, and other worthy lessons. Sports can build egos, and can create in a child a bone-deep self-confidence that carries over into other things the child does. And finally, learning early to enjoy sports can have the best possible influence on the development of your child's life-fitness habits by sugarcoating the pill of exercise.

On the other side of this coin, few experiences in a child's life can be as damaging as a bad experience with team sports—as destructive of confidence, as tough on the ego and self-esteem, as unrewarding, as un-fun. And such an experience can be, and often is, the *worst* possible influence on the development of good fitness habits by turning a child off exercise and physical activity, sometimes for life.

And who determines which kind of experience your child will have with team sports? It could be a school physical education teacher, a Little League coach, even other children. But if you are smart, it will be you, and only you. Just as *you* must control your child's physical development and education in the home and insist on quality physical and health education in the school, so must you take the ultimate responsibility for guiding your child toward the *right* kind of team sport participation—either at school or in the community—and away from the wrong kind.

And what are the right and wrong kinds of team sports participation for kids ages six through ten? Here are a few guidelines:

▶ Never push your child into any sport solely because *you* want him or her to play it. For example, I would never expect my daughters to be bodybuilding champions down the line. Talk over the pros and cons of various sports, team and individual, with your child and let him or her decide which, if any, to take up. Ideally, kids should begin with one or more of the "individual," life-fitness sports, like swimming or biking, and then move into team sports.

▶ Don't let your child enter into a sport before he or she is developmentally ready to play and enjoy it. Kids develop physically and emotionally at different speeds. If your seven-year-old boy, for example, is a little slow developing eye-foot coordination and agility, and has a hard time concentrating on plays and game strategies, he is probably not ready to enjoy playing organized soccer.

▶ A sport, like fitness, *has to be fun* for a kid to stick with it. Encourage your child to try out as many team and individual sports as possible, looking for the ones he or she has fun playing.

▶ Any school or community team sports program that emphasizes winning over fun, over general participation (by *every* kid who wants to be on the team), and over good sportsmanship should be avoided like the plague. There is plenty of time for your child to get really skilled at a sport and to become an intense competitor, if that is going to happen. Between ages six and ten, he or she should enjoy, participate in, and improve at his or her own speed, and learn how to win and lose fairly, generously, and gracefully. Achieving "personal best" performances should be the really meaningful goals for kids this age.

▶ Also avoid programs that have too much adult interference in them, either from over-zealous coaches or parents. Sports should belong to the kids at this age. Whatever coaching your child *is* receiving should be skilled and knowledgeable.

▶ According to Thomas Fahey, author of *Competitive Sports and Your Child*, "Five- to ten-year-olds should belong to organized teams only if those teams provide an atmosphere for learning a variety of movement fundamentals and for developing a love of the sport." That sums it up pretty well.

To evaluate how a particular team sport at your child's school or in your community meets these guidelines, you should begin by having a conversation with the coach. Ask him or her to describe how the team program your child is about to enter fits into the guidelines given above. What is his philosophy of coaching? Will everyone on the team get more or less equal playing

time? Is the team coed, and if not, why not? How important is it to the coach that the kids have fun? (Vince Lombardi is supposed to have said about football, "Winning isn't the main thing, it's the only thing." Well with kids' sports, fun is "the only thing," and your child's coach should agree with that.) What will be the fitness benefits of playing on this team, if any? Does the coach teach sportsmanship? What is the injury risk in this sport? Etcetera.

You might also want to talk with a few parents whose kids have been, or are, on this team and have been coached by this coach. If you and your child decide to give the team a try, keep up with how he or she is doing. (Is she having fun? Is he getting to play regularly?) Show your support by going to games, and praise your child's effort and improvement rather than performance; leave the coaching to the coach; and, despite the temptations, *don't* turn into a "sports mom" or "sports dad," pitching fits on the sidelines and yelling insults at the other team during games.

Though the right kind of organized team sports can play a valuable role in your child's development and contribute significantly to the laying of a good life-fitness foundation during ages six through ten, team sports are certainly not necessary to either that development or that foundation. If your child doesn't want to play team sports, or plays one for a while and drops out, fine. Play golf with him; introduce her to tennis; take a karate or aquatics class together; or a canoe trip; or go cross-country skiing. If *your* attitude toward sports is that they are, above all else, enjoyable corollaries to a healthy, energetic, fun life, that attitude will rub off on your child, who will in turn find the individual sports that he or she can enjoy in that same way.

In any case, if you have put the rest of this book to use, your child will never have to depend on sports to get or stay fit—and that is something you can be proud of.

APPENDIX a

aerobic exercises and games

I. aerobic exercises

NOTE: Any of these exercises should be done continuously for fifteen minutes if you are six or seven, or for twenty minutes if you are eight, nine, or ten—each time you do your aerobic workout. Don't forget to warm up before aerobic exercise and to cool down after it.

▶ **Walking (at a brisk pace, swinging the arms)**

▶ **Jogging/running**

▶ **Swimming**

▶ **Cycling**

▶ **Rowing or canoe paddling**

▶ **Cross-country skiing**

▶ **Aerobic exercise classes or aerobic dance**

▶ **Rope skipping**

▶ **Ice or roller skating (done continuously)**

Sports such as soccer, basketball, wrestling, martial arts, handball, racquetball, squash, and singles tennis can provide good aerobic workouts if you play them continuously (without stopping and with as few pauses in your movement as possible).

II. aerobic games

▶ Be sure to warm up for five minutes before playing these games strenuously, and to cool down for five minutes after your play period. Warm up by walking, walking in a circle, walking and swinging your arms, doing jumping jacks, or stretching. Cool down with stretches and/or walking.

▶ To get the best aerobic benefit from these games, you should keep moving; *all the time* (that is, keep your legs moving; try kicking or jogging in place even when going over rules or while going from one game to another).

▶ Don't let anyone get overly competitive about these games—the point is that everyone is a winner just by getting fit.

▶ You can do a number of games in a session, one right after another, or stick with just one. Find out what "works" for your sessions.

▶ Make up your own aerobic games—you'll find it's easy and fun.

▶ The games given for six- and seven-year-olds that are asterisked may also be enjoyed by kids eight, nine, and ten years of age.

games for ages six and seven

truck driver Someone stands behind you with her hands on your shoulders and "drives" you around the yard or house. The driver can say "speed up" or "slow down," and can drive you in different gears: a run, a fast walk, a hop, etc. After three minutes, swap positions and you become the driver.

leapfrog Set up a goal line about thirty yards away from where you and a partner are standing. Now you and your partner take turns leapfrogging each other out to the goal and back.

frog jump Everyone who is playing pretends to be a frog by squatting down and jumping. Take turns calling out different jumps—side to side, forward and backward, jump and clap, jump toward a goal line, jump and croak.

back to back Stand back to back with a partner and hook your arms together. One of you calls out a movement (running forward or backward together, leg kicks, side hops) and you do five of them. Then the other partner calls out a different movement and you do five of those. Keep taking turns calling out different movements and see how many movements you can come up with.

balloon free-for-all You can play this with one to four or five people. Blow up twice as many balloons as there are people and try to keep them all in the air by hitting them with Ping-Pong paddles or your hands.

*tag There are all kinds of tag games and you can adapt tag to any size playing field and play it with two to twenty people. Someone is "It" until that person, chases down and tags another person, who then becomes "It" until he tags someone else, and so on. You can play "rainy day tag" in a big open room by crawling or hopping on one foot instead of running.

*nerf ball tag To play tag with a Nerf or other foam ball, the person designated "It" has to throw the ball and hit someone with it for that person to become "It."

*tail tag In this good two-person variation of tag, one partner puts a bandana or handkerchief in his back pocket so that it hangs down like a tail. The other partner has to chase the person with the tail until she can grab it and put it in *her* back pocket. Then partner A tries to take the tail back from B, and so on.

*steal the ball The same idea as tail tag, but here, one partner runs around throwing up a ball and catching it and tries to keep it away from the other partner. Whoever has the ball has to keep throwing it up and catching it, and should not just hold on to it and run.

arnold says This can be played with two to ten people. One person is "Arnold" for three minutes, then someone else for three minutes, until everyone gets a turn. Whoever is Arnold tells everyone else what to do and does it with them: "Arnold says, 'Do ten sit-ups' "; "Arnold says, 'Run forward' "; "Arnold says, 'Jog in place' "—and some other exercises Arnold can say are skip, do push-ups, do jumping jacks, run in place, run backward. Each exercise should be done for ten to fifteen seconds, then Arnold should "say" another exercise.

games for ages eight, nine, and ten

keep away This game is played with two teams and a ball. Each team can be small—only one person; or large—as many as ten. Your playing field can be a yard, a field, even a big, open room. Or, three people can play Keep Away by putting one person between two others, who then try to keep a ball away from the person in the middle by throwing or kicking it around or over him. When the person in the middle catches the ball, his place is taken by the person who threw or kicked it. In two-man Keep Away one person tries to keep a ball or a flag away from the other one (see Tail Tag and Steal the Ball, above). In Keep Away with teams of two or more, Team A passes a ball around while Team B tries to intercept it. When they do, Team B tries to keep the ball away from Team A.

ultimate frisbee You can play this with two to six people on a team. Create two goal lines fifty to one hundred yards apart. One team starts at its goal line with the Frisbee and runs up the field passing it (no player can hold the disc between passes for more than three seconds) back and forth and trying to cross the other team's goal line without having the disc intercepted or batted down to the ground. If the Frisbee is batted down or intercepted, the other team takes possession of it at that point and tries to score going in the opposite direction.

relay races There are all kinds of relay races and most of them are fun for kids and adults to play together. You'll need two teams of two or more people per team. Make a starting line and a goal line (the two lines can be as far apart or as close as you want). The first players on each team race each other to the goal line (by running, running while dribbling a basketball or soccer ball, hopping, rolling, somersaulting, running backward) and back to the starting line. As soon as a player returns to the starting line, he tags the next player on his team (or gives him the ball) and that player then takes off on the course. The team that wins is the one whose last player finishes before the last player on the other team. Have everyone waiting at the starting line jog in place until their time comes to race the course.

station training courses In Sweden many of the parks have popular station training fitness courses where people run from station to station and at each station do a different exercise. You can create your own version of this in your backyard, playground, or in a nearby park. Create a course with four to ten "stations" (a station is just a flat area big enough to exercise in) connected by "runs" (or jogs or walks) of various distances (for example, you might run fifty yards between Stations 1 and 2, then skip twenty yards to Station 3, then jog a hundred yards to Station 4, then sprint fifty yards back to Station 1). At each station you do a different set of exercises—maybe twenty sit-ups at Station 1, forty jumping jacks at Station 2, ten push-ups at Station 3, and twenty seconds of jumping rope at Station 4—before running (or jogging, skipping) on to the next station.

one-on-one Two people can play one-on-one soccer or basketball without a goal or a basket. For both games draw two goal lines at either end of a field, yard, or playground. One goal line "belongs" to Player A, the other to Player B. One player, say Player A, starts out dribbling a basketball or soccer ball (with his or her feet) and tries to cross Player B's goal line. Player B tries to take the ball away, and if he does, he tries to cross Player A's goal line. If Player A does cross Player B's goal line, the ball automatically goes to B and vice versa.

APPENDIX B

motor-skills drills and games

I. games

All sports and games that require bodily movement will help develop motor skills, and the more sports and active games a child aged six through ten tries out, the better it is for his or her skills development. Here are a few games that most people can play at home with just two (an adult and a child) or three people (two adults and a child, or two children and an adult).

one-on-one basketball

one-on-one nerf baseball One person bats and after a hit tries to make it to a single base and back for a home run before the other person, the pitcher, can "tag" the batter out by touching him with the ball. After three outs, batter and pitcher change places. Kickball can be played the same way.

one-on-one or three-way soccer-dribbling keep away

one-on-one or three-way tag

one-on-one or three-way tag on skates

three-way keep away with a ball

three-way keep away with hockey puck on ice with skates and hockey sticks

three-way softball throw Kids position themselves roughly in a triangle position about twenty to thirty feet away from one another, but keep running. The person who has the ball can throw only to a person who is in motion, giving one child practice at throwing to a moving target, and the other child practice at getting to the ball, stopping, and positioning himself to catch the ball. Each player should touch the ball on every third throw, so that everyone gets equal practice with throwing and catching.

three-way kickball A kicker, a pitcher, and a fielder; whoever puts the kicker out takes his place.

II. skill drills for ages six and seven

NOTE: The drills here that have an asterisk beside them are also appropriate for kids eight through ten.

toe stands (for balance) With your hands on your hips, stand up on your tiptoes for five to fifteen seconds. Then do it with your arms out to your sides, then your arms held straight over your head. Now try all three of these toe stands again, this time with your eyes closed, and try to hold each one for five to fifteen seconds without losing your balance.

*the stork stand (for balance) Stand on your right foot with your hands on your hips and your left foot held against the inside of your right knee (like a stork). Try to hold this position for fifteen seconds. Then do it on your left leg. Then do it on each leg while holding your arms in different positions—out to your sides, over your head. Then do it on each leg with your eyes closed (the Blind Stork Stand). Try to work up to doing the Blind Stork Stand for fifteen seconds on each leg without losing your balance.

*walking the plank (for balance, balance stabilization, multilimb coordination, eyefoot coordination) Lay an eight-foot long, two-by-four-inch plank out on the ground or floor and practice walking it, placing one foot directly in front of the other, without coming off the plank. Then practice walking the plank sideways by crossing one foot over the other; then on tiptoes; then walk the plank, make a 180-degree turn, and walk back. Finally, practice walking the plank backward and then with your eyes closed. Important: make sure you master walking the plank in one way before you go on to another.

*tire and plank walk (for balance, balance stabilization, eye-foot coordination, multi-limb coordination) Get four eight-foot-long, two-by-four-inch boards and four old tires and lay them out in your yard in a pattern as shown:

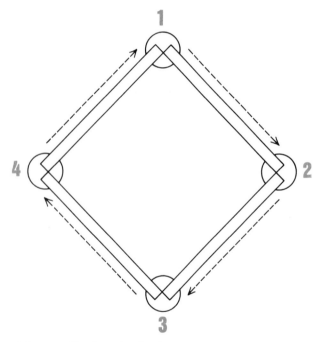

Now walk the planks from position one to two, to three, to four, and back to one again. After you can do that three times without a foot touching the ground, try it by going from one to four to three to two and back to one. Try both routes sideways, on tiptoes, or backward.

catch and toss (eye-hand coordination, visual tracking) Get your mom or dad to toss balls to you, then you toss them back. Start with a fairly big ball like a kickball, with the two of you standing only a few feet apart. Then as you get better at catching and tossing, move farther apart and play with smaller balls—Nerf softballs, footballs, or tennis balls.

*soccer trap and kick (eye-foot coordination, whole-body coordination, agility) Play the soccer version of toss and catch by kicking a soccer ball back and forth and "catching," or trapping, it with your feet.

nerf softball hitting (eye-hand coordination, visual tracking, multilimb coordination) Have someone pitch (underhand) a Nerf softball to you and practice hitting it with the Nerf bat. Or practice throwing the ball up in the air yourself and hitting it. You can do the same thing with a tennis ball and kid's racquet.

*basketball dribble (eye-hand coordination, multilimb coordination) Practice dribbling a junior-size basketball. Practice with each hand while standing still at first, then while walking, then while running.

*juggling (eye-hand coordination) Hold a tennis ball in each hand. Throw the ball in the left hand to the right hand and vice versa, simultaneously. If you get good at this, you may want to go on to juggling three balls at the same time.

*yardstick reaction-time drill (eye-hand coordination, reaction time) Reaction time is how long it takes you to respond physically to a visual stimulus. It is an extremely important skill in almost all sports. This drill helps improve your reaction time. Sit in a chair with your forearms lying flat and your right or left hand held as shown in the illustration. Keep your thumb and forefinger absolutely level and don't move your hand off the table during the drill. Someone should hold the yardstick at the thirty-six-inch end above your hand so that the one-inch end is level with the top of your thumb and forefinger in the gap created between them. When you say "go," the person holding the yardstick has five seconds to drop it (he or she can drop it any time during those five seconds). When the yardstick is dropped, you catch it by closing your thumb and forefinger as quickly as you can *after* the yardstick has been dropped. Now read the number of inches where your fingers closed on the yardstick. One to five inches is excellent, six to ten inches is good, eleven to fifteen inches is fair. Do the drill until you can catch the yardstick with both hands at less than the ten-inch mark.

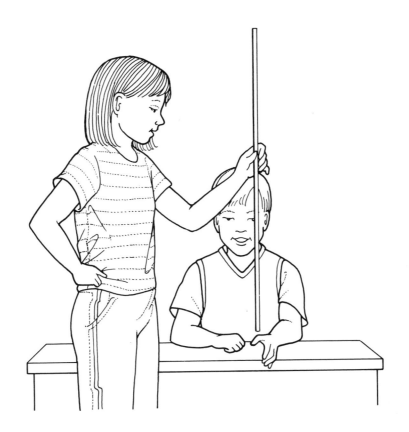

*nerf ball accuracy throw (eye-hand coordination, multilimb coordination, aiming) Lay out a square of sticks or tape that is two feet on each side. Stand ten feet away from the square if you are six or seven, twenty feet away if you are eight, nine, or ten. Now throw a Nerf or other foam ball so that it lands in the square on the fly. Work up to where you can throw the ball into the square eight out of ten times, then move five feet farther away and practice from there.

*soccer ball dribbling (eye-foot coordination, balance, whole-body coordination, agility, foot speed) Practice dribbling a soccer ball (kicking it from foot to foot), standing still at first, then at a walk, and finally at a slow run.

*agility runs (whole-body coordination, balance, agility) Set up milk containers, old tires, chairs, or whatever, in the patterns shown in the illustration. You can run, hop, or skip through these courses, or have races through them (pretend they are ski slalom courses). You can also reverse the directions of the courses and make them any size you want.

course no. 1

course no. 2

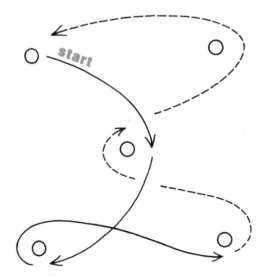

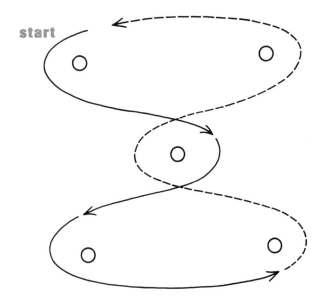

start

*jumping rope (whole-body coordination, balance, agility, foot speed)
Jumping rope is great exercise and also a great skill builder. Start with a simple two-foot
hop over the rope and then develop other skills such as skipping over the rope, jumping
on one foot at a time, or crossing your arms.

skill drills for ages eight, nine, and ten

the turning stork (balance, balance stabilization) This is a more difficult
version of the Stork Stand given for younger kids. This one lets you practice stabilizing
your body's balance during movement, an important skill in most sports. You should do
this in socks on a slick floor. Stand in the position described in the Stork Stand, hands on
hips, standing on either leg. Stand for five seconds, then swivel on the ball of your foot
180 degrees to your right. After five more seconds of standing, swivel 180 degrees more
to your right, back to your original position. Stand for five seconds in that position, then
make two 180-degree swivels to your left. When you get to the point where you can do
four or five of these rotations to either side, try them with your eyes closed.

**the four-ball throw (eye-hand coordination, aiming accuracy,
multilimb coordination)** You and a partner stand facing each other, about ten
feet apart, each of you holding a tennis ball in each hand. Using an underhand toss,
simultaneously throw the balls in your right hands to each other; then the balls in your

left hands; then throw the ball in your right hand to your partner's left hand as he does the same thing; then the ball in your left hand to his right as he does the same thing. As you get good at this, move farther apart.

nerf football tire throw (eye-hand coordination, aiming accuracy, visual tracking) Hang an old tire from a tree limb by a rope so that it hangs about four feet off the ground. Stand about twelve feet from the tire and get someone to start it swinging slowly. Practice throwing a Nerf or other foam football through the tire while it is swinging. As you get better at this, you can move farther back and/or swing the tire faster. Many a top NFL quarterback has developed his passing skills with this tire drill.

tire run (balance, foot speed, multilimb coordination, eye-foot coordination, agility) Set up old tires in the pattern shown in the illustration, and practice running (slowly at first) through them. Run the course with your left foot going into the tires on your left, and your right foot going into the tires on your right. Then run in a normal way (one foot ahead of the other) through one line of tires and back through the other line.

Start   Finish

soccer dribble obstacle course (eye-foot coordination, balance, whole-body coordination, agility) Set up a course like one of the ones shown in the illustration, using old tires, milk cartons, or some such, and practice dribbling a soccer ball through the course with your feet. Vary the dimensions of the course (the closer the objects are to each other, the harder it is) and experiment with your own course designs.

course no. 1

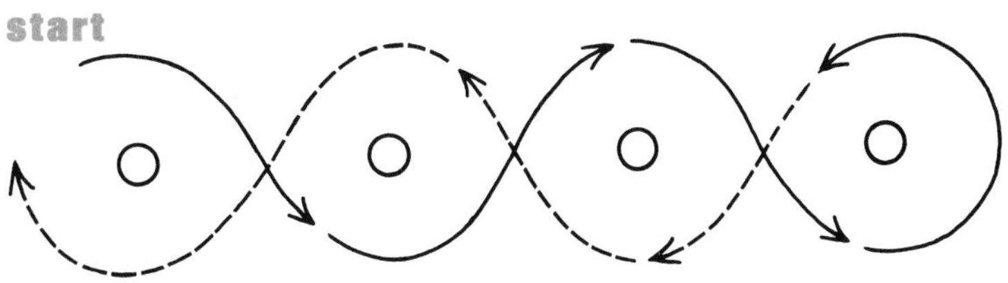

start

course no. 2

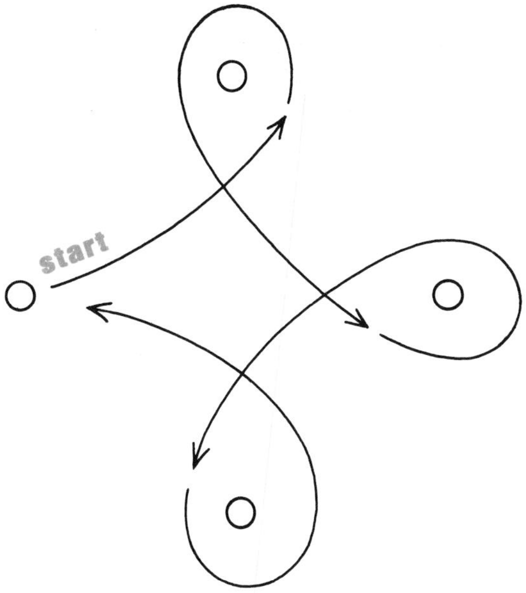

start

course no. 3

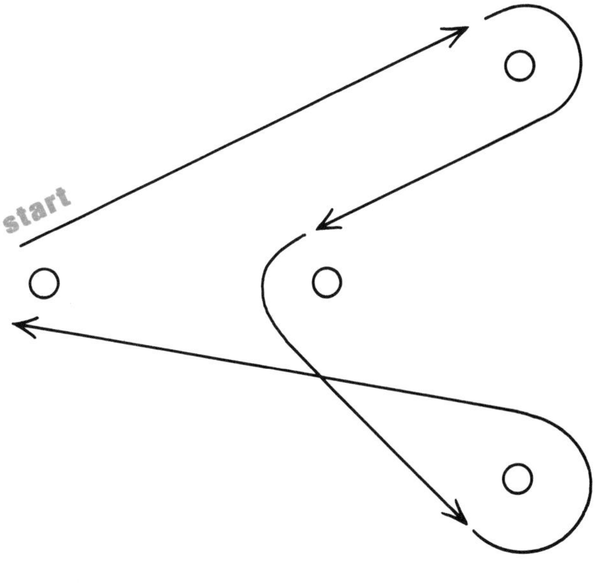

start

basketball dribble obstacle course (eye-hand coordination, whole-body coordination, balance, agility, dexterity) Practice dribbling a basketball through one or more of the courses shown for the soccer dribble or make up your own course.

bicycle obstacle course (whole-body coordination, balance, balance stabilization) Biking, particularly BMX and off-road mountain biking, is a great skill builder. Make the course with old tires, as shown in the illustration, and practice riding through it both from left to right and from right to left. As you get better at it, move the tires closer together.

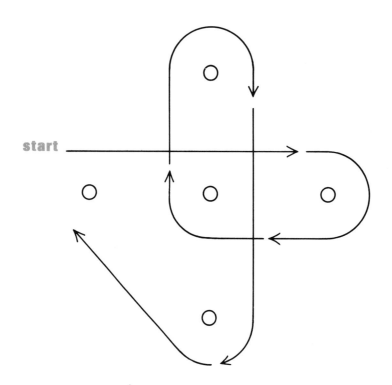

hexagonal jump (balance, whole-body coordination, agility, foot speed) This is one of the best overall skill developers there is, and it's used as a test by the Austrian Ski Team to determine alpine skiing ability. With two-inch masking tape, create the hexagon shown in the illustration (twenty-two inches per side) on a hard, flat surface. Stand in the middle of the hexagon facing side F, as you must for the duration of the drill. Jump out of the hexagon over side A and immediately back into the hexagon. Then, continuing to face side F, jump over side B and back into the hexagon, over side C and back in, over side D and back in, over side E and back in, and finally over side F and back in for one complete revolution. Your feet should not touch any one of the lines. Practice going around once perfectly, then twice, then three times, as fast as you can. Some top junior alpine skiers can do three complete revolutions without touching a line with their feet in nine seconds. See if you can work down to that!

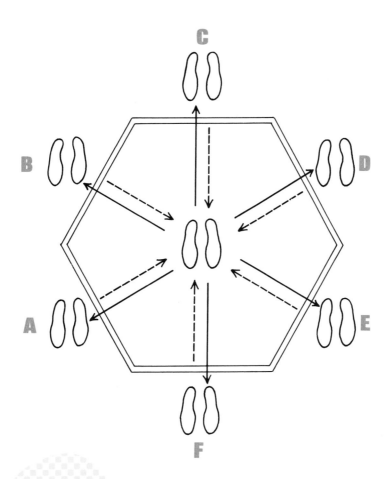

APPENDIX C

flexibility exercises

▶ Remember—no bouncing!

▶ Don't hold your breath as you stretch.

▶ The exercises that are asterisked are fine for six- and seven-year-olds before and after aerobic activity.

*calf stretch Stand six to ten inches from a wall and lean on it with your elbows or forearms. Rest your head on your hands. Bend the knee of your forward leg and stretch the other leg out behind you as far as you can and still keep your heel on the ground. Hold the stretch for ten seconds. Then stretch the other leg.

*thigh and knee stretch Stand a few inches from a wall and put your right hand on the wall. Hold the top of your right foot in your left hand and gently pull your heel up toward your buttocks. Hold for thirty seconds, then reverse your position and stretch the left thigh and knee.

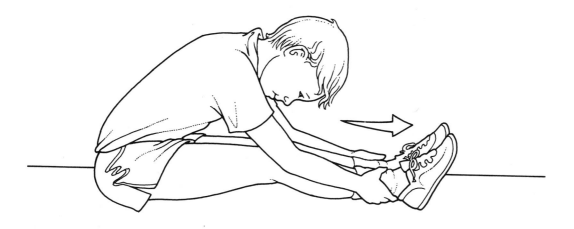

*hamstring and hip stretch Sitting on the floor with your legs slightly bent at the knees, grasp your calves and slide your hands forward toward your ankles as far as you can comfortably go. Hold the stretch for ten seconds.

two-part arm and shoulder stretch
With both arms held overhead, gently pull the elbow of your right arm behind your head, letting your forearm and hand hang down your back, until you feel the stretch in your shoulder and the back of your arm. Hold for ten seconds. Then pull your right elbow *across* your chest toward your left shoulder as far as it will comfortably go and hold that stretch for ten seconds. Now do the same two stretches with your left arm.

*arms, shoulder, and chest stretch Interlace your fingers behind your back and lift both arms behind you until you feel a stretch in your arms, shoulders, and chest. Keep your chest out and your chin in. Hold for ten seconds.

arms and upper-back stretch Interlace your fingers over your head and face your palms upward. Push your arms up and back until you feel a stretch in your upper back and the backs of your arms. Hold for ten seconds.

*side and back stretch Extend both arms over your head and clasp your hands together. Bend slowly to the right, using your right hand to pull your left arm over your head and down toward the ground, until you feel a stretch from the back of your arm down through your side and spine. Don't overstretch—just go as far as it is comfortable, and hold for six seconds.

*back stretch Lie flat on your back. Grasp your right knee with both hands and pull it up and in toward your chest as far as is comfortable. Hold it there for ten seconds, keeping your head flat on the floor. Then do the same thing with your left leg. Then pull both knees into your chest and hold them there for ten seconds.

upper back and neck stretch Standing up, lace your fingers behind your head and slowly pull your head forward and down toward your chest until you feel a stretch at the back of your neck. Hold for five seconds. Do this stretch three times, holding each for five seconds.

*entire body stretch Lie flat on your back with your legs two or three inches apart and your arms lying over your head, also two or three inches apart. Now stretch your arms out in the direction they are pointing and, at the same time, your feet in the opposite direction, as if you were trying to lengthen your body. Hold for five seconds, then relax. Repeat three or four times.

hamstring (back of the thigh) stretch A good advanced stretch for running, biking, and sports. Sit with the sole of your left foot touching the inside of your right thigh. Your right leg should be straight out, with the foot upright. Now slowly bend forward from the hips toward your right foot, sliding your hands down your right leg to the ankle, until you feel a slight stretch in the back of your right leg. Don't push your head forward as you bend into the stretch. Hold that position for ten seconds, then bend a little more forward from the hips until you feel another tug. Hold that final position for fifteen more seconds. Then reverse your position and do the same stretch with the left leg.

groin and lower-back stretch Another great stretch to do before strenuous exercise. Sit on the floor and put the soles of your feet together in front of you. Holding on to your toes, gently lean forward from the hips until you feel a stretch in your groin and lower back. Don't push your head and shoulders forward to initiate the stretch, but lean forward *from the hips*. If you have a problem leaning forward, move your feet farther out in front of you. Hold the stretch for fifteen seconds, relax, and do it twice more for fifteen seconds apiece.

APPENDIX D

strength and muscular endurance exercises

for the stomach muscles

sit-ups Sitting on the floor with your knees bent, place your feet under some stationary object. Cross your arms over your chest, with your hands on your shoulders. Now lower your upper body until your lower back touches the floor and sit back up for one repetition. Do these slowly and fluidly (don't jerk your upper body upward). Do as many repetitions as you comfortably can, and increase your repetitions as the exercise gets easier for you, working up to forty to fifty. Do one to three sets.

crunches This version of the sit-up puts no pressure at all on the lower back. Lie on your back with your legs bent steeply at the knees and elevated, and your hands on your hips. Rolling your shoulders and head off the floor, touch your chin to your chest and "crunch," or tense, your stomach muscles as you do it. Hold the crunch for a count of three, then relax and return to

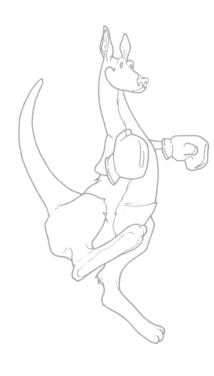

your original position for one repetition. Work up to twenty-five to thirty repetitions. Do one to three sets.

knee-ups This exercise is for the lower abdominal muscles. Lie flat on the floor with your hands underneath your buttocks. Holding your legs together, bend your knees and raise them six inches off the floor. Bring your knees in toward your chest as far as you can, then straighten your legs slowly for one repetition. Work up to twenty-five to thirty repetitions. Do one to three sets.

seated twists These are good for strengthening the side muscles of the waist (intercostals and obliques), and also for increasing spinal flexibility. Sit on a bench, stool, or chair and hold your arms out by your sides at shoulder level. Twist at the waist to your right, bringing your arms and upper body around as far as they will comfortably go. Then come back to your starting position and twist in the other direction. Alternate twenty-five repetitions to each side. Do one to three sets. This is also a great warm-up exercise.

for the leg muscles

Find a sturdy stool, bench, or box about the same height as a stairway step and stand in front of it. Step up on the object with your right foot (*step,* don't heave or jump up—let your thigh muscles bring you up). Now step down and step back up with your left foot. Step down again for one repetition with each foot. Work up to thirty to forty step-ups with each foot. Do one to three sets. This is good for the frontal thigh muscles and the buttocks.

lunges Lunges strengthen the upper legs and hips and also improve balance and hip flexibility. Stand with your feet together and your arms held straight out to your sides for balance. Now step forward two or three feet with your right leg and sink onto it until you touch the knee of your left leg to the floor (if this is hard, don't sink so far). Come back up to your original position for one repetition with that leg. Now do the same thing on your left leg. Alternate legs up to twenty-five lunges per leg. Do one to three sets.

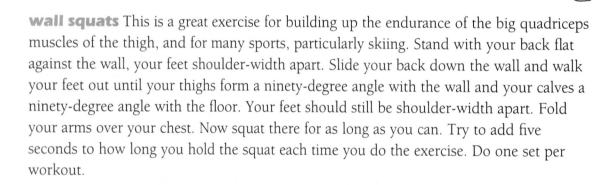

wall squats This is a great exercise for building up the endurance of the big quadriceps muscles of the thigh, and for many sports, particularly skiing. Stand with your back flat against the wall, your feet shoulder-width apart. Slide your back down the wall and walk your feet out until your thighs form a ninety-degree angle with the wall and your calves a ninety-degree angle with the floor. Your feet should still be shoulder-width apart. Fold your arms over your chest. Now squat there for as long as you can. Try to add five seconds to how long you hold the squat each time you do the exercise. Do one set per workout.

calf raises Find a thick book or piece of four-by-four-inch board. Stand on it, with your feet a few inches apart, so that only the balls of your feet and the first couple of inches of your instep are on the object and your heels are dropped down as far as they will go. It helps to have something in front of you to hold on to. Now stand up slowly on the balls of your feet until your calf muscles contract fully. Hold that position for a count of five—feeling the contraction in your calves—then let your heels drop back down slowly to their original position for one repetition. Work up to twenty-five repetitions, held for five seconds each, and do one to three sets. This exercise can also be done one leg at a time, which makes it harder.

for the chest muscles

push-ups Probably the best all-around upper-body strength exercise there is, push-ups work not only the chest but the shoulders and triceps (back of the arms) muscles as well. Lie flat on your stomach, your feet on their toes, hands directly under your shoulders and level with them. Lift your waist from the floor so only your chest is touching. Now, keeping your head down and your back straight, push up until your arms are fully extended. Go back down to your original position for one repetition. Work up to twenty-five reps and do one to three sets. Each time you do push-ups, try to do one more.

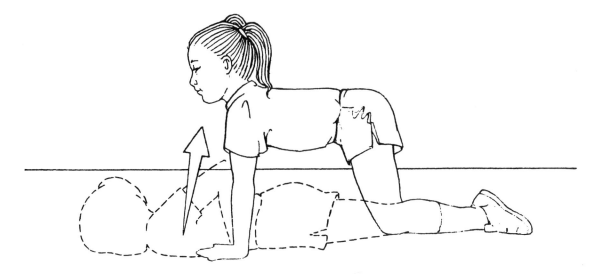

modified push-ups If you can't do the exercise above, substitute this one. Start with your chin touching the floor, your weight resting on your hands and knees, your hands approximately shoulder-width apart. Push up and back, keeping your back and waist in a straight line, to a crawling position. Work up on repetitions of these until you are strong enough to do the normal push-ups described above. Do one to three sets.

push-offs Find a table, bench, dresser, wall—something about half your height. Stand in front of it, with your feet three feet away and a foot apart. Place your hands on the object, spacing them a foot to two feet wider than your shoulders. Holding your back straight, lower (don't drop) your upper body so that your chest touches the object, then push slowly back up for one repetition. The farther your feet are away from the object, the harder the exercise is. Work up to twenty-five to thirty of these and do one to three sets.

alternate flies and pull-overs with books This is a good exercise for strengthening the chest and upper abdominals, and also for upper-body flexibility. Lie on your back on the floor, knees bent, holding two books of equal weight (or soup cans, or

other) directly over your chest. With your arms slightly bent, lower the books out to the sides until they go below your chest, then bring your arms back up in a slight bow, as though you were hugging something, until the books touch. Then, with the books together, lower your arms back behind your head as far as they will go and, using your chest and upper stomach muscles, pull them back up to a vertical position for one full

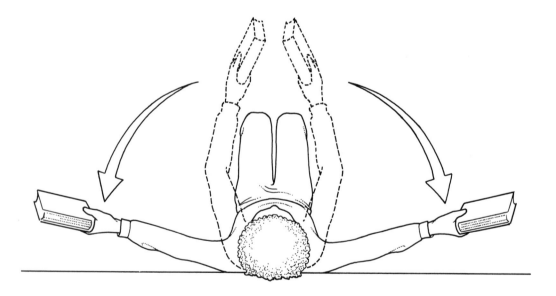

repetition of the exercise. Try to do the four movements smoothly and at the maximum stretch. As you get stronger, you can use heavier books. Work up to twenty reps, and do one to three sets.

for the back muscles

lower-back extensions This exercise strengthens the lower-back muscles and buttocks, and is also good for lower-back flexibility. Lie on your stomach and chest with your head held off the floor and your arms lifted behind you and to the sides. Lift your legs and upper body toward each other, leaving only your stomach and hips on the floor, as far as they will comfortably go, and hold that position for a count of three. Then go back to your original position for one repetition. Work up to twenty reps, and do one set. Adults with lower-back problems should be careful with this exercise.

modified pull-ups These pull-ups strengthen the muscles of the upper back. To do them you will need a couple of stable objects about two feet high—a couple of chairs or tables—and a broomstick or some other kind of sturdy pole. Arrange the pole as shown in the illustration. Make sure the pole is firmly in place. Lie on your back and take a wide grip on the pole. Keeping your heels on the floor, pull your chest as close as you can to the pole, then let yourself down slowly for one repetition. Keep your back straight as you do these and let your back muscles do the pulling. Work up to ten repetitions. Do one to three sets.

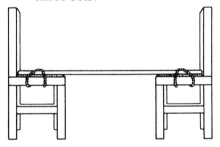 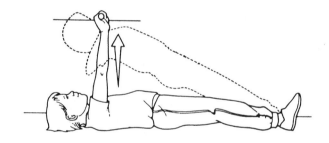

for the shoulder muscles

shoulder push-offs This works the important deltoid muscles of the shoulders. Find a table, bench, or chair that is around hip height. Standing with feet a couple of feet apart and about three feet from the object, place your hands on the object, spacing them a little wider than your shoulders. Now bend at the waist so that your back goes flat and on the same level as your outstretched arms. Let your head come in to touch the object, then push off from it, keeping your back level, back to your

original position. If you're doing this exercise correctly, you'll feel it in your shoulders. You can make the exercise more difficult by moving your feet farther away from the object. Work up to twenty repetitions, and do one to three sets.

for the muscles of the hands, wrists, and fingers

Carry a soft rubber ball about two inches in diameter around with you everywhere you go (the ball used for racquetball is perfect), and do a hand-squeeze workout with it two or three times a day. Squeeze the ball with your right hand until that hand is too tired to squeeze anymore, then squeeze it with your left hand, then your right hand again, then your left, for one full workout. Strong hands and wrists come in "handy" in all sorts of ways.

for the arm muscles

pull-ups These are good for the biceps muscles of the arms and also for muscles in your shoulders, chest, and back. Do pull-ups with your hands in a forward grip and a little farther apart than shoulder width. Pull smoothly up until your chin reaches the bar, then let yourself down until your arms are straight for one repetition. Work up to ten repetitions, and do one to two sets each workout.

dips This is for the triceps muscles at the rear of the arms. Stand as shown in the illustration, your hands on a chair placed against the wall. Lower buttocks down toward the floor until your chest is on a plane with your hands, then push yourself smoothly back up to starting position, using the muscles in the backs of your arms. Work up to one to three sets of twelve repetitions, and if this exercise gets too easy for you, do it with your feet elevated in a chair, as shown in the other illustration.

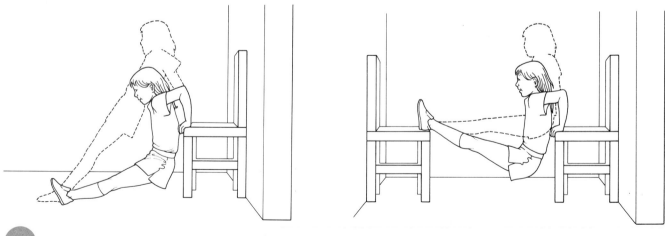

The following is a list of works consulted in the research of these books:

COOPER, KENNETH H., M.D. *Kid Fitness: A Complete Shape-Up Program from Birth Through High School.* New York: Bantam, 1991.

AMERICAN ACADEMY OF PEDIATRICS, *Caring for Your Baby and Child, Birth to Age 5.* Edited by STEVEN P. SHELOV, M.D., F.A.A.P. (editor-in-chief), and ROBERT E. HANNEMANN, M.D., F.A.A.P. (associate medical editor). New York: Bantam, 1991.

ANDERSON, BOB. *Stretching.* Bolinas, Calif.: Shelter Publications, Inc., 1980.

ARNOT, ROBERT, M.D., and CHARLES GAINES. *Sports Talent.* New York: Viking Penguin, 1984.

EISENBERG, ARLENE, HEIDI E. MURKOFF, and SANDEE E. HATHAWAY, B.S.N. *What to Expect the First Year.* New York: Workman, 1989.

FIRKALY, SUSAN TATE. *Into the Mouths of Babes.* White Hall, Va.: Betterway Publications, Inc., 1984.

GAINES, CHARLES, and GEORGE BUTLER. *Staying Hard.* New York: Kenan Press, 1988.

GLOVER, BOB, and JACK SHEPHERD. *The Family Fitness Handbook.* New York: The Penguin Group, 1989.

KUNTZLEMAN, DR. CHARLES T. *Healthy Kids for Life.* New York: Simon and Schuster, 1988.

KUNTZLEMAN, CHARLES, and BETH and MICHAEL and GAIL McGLYNN. *Aerobics with Fun.* Reston, Va.: AAHPERD, 1991.

LEACH, PENELOPE, PH.D. *Your Baby & Child from Birth to Age Five.* New York: Alfred A. Knopf, 1990.

McCOY, KATHY, and CHARLES WIBBELSMAN, M.D. *The New Teenage Body Book.* Los Angeles: The Body Press, 1987.

McINALLY, PAT. *Moms & Dads, Kids & Sports.* New York: Charles Scribners Sons, 1988.

MICHELI, LYLE J., M.D. *Sportswise: An Essential Guide for Young Athletes, Parents, and Coaches.* Boston: Houghton Mifflin, 1990.

ORLICK, TERRY. *The Cooperative Sports & Games Book.* New York: Pantheon Books, 1978.

PETRAY, DR. CLAYRE K., and SANDRA L. BLAZER. *Health-Related Physical Fitness: Concepts and Activities for Elementary School Children.* Edina, Minn.: Bellwether Press, 1987.

ROWLAND, THOMAS W. *Exercise and Children's Health.* Champaign, Ill.: Human Kinetics Books, 1990.

First and foremost, special thanks to Jane Forrestal Ellsworth. Thanks also to Stephen Lesko, graduate assistant at Springfield College, Springfield, Mass.; Dr. Mimi Murray, Springfield College; Donna Israel, nutrition expert at Cooper Institute; Janice M. O'Donnell, NHAHPERD; Diane Rappa, NHAHPERD; Tom Walton, physical education teacher at Rundlett Junior High School, Concord, N.H.; Professor Vern Seefeldt, Director, Youth Sports Institute, Michigan State University; Suzie Boos, RightStart Program, Children's Hospital of Illinois; Becky Davang, Kids' Aerobics, Sugar Land, Tex.; Susan Astor, President, Playorena, Roslyn Heights, N.Y.; Doug Moss, Marketing Specialist, Gymboree; Doug Curry, President (1991), MHAHPERD (Michigan); Sharon Nicosia, physical education teacher, Beaver Meadow Elementary School, Concord, N.H.; Beth Kirkpatrick, physical education teacher, Tilford Middle School, Vinton, Iowa, and past recipient of the Teacher of the Year Award from AAHPERD; Lani Graham, NASPE (part of AAHPERD); Lyle J. Micheli, M.D., Boston Children's Hospital; Dr. Charles T. Kuntzleman; Jill Werman; Louise McCormick, Plymouth State College, Plymouth, N.H.; President's Council on Physical Fitness and Sports, Washington, D.C.; American Alliance for Health, Physical Education, Recreation and Dance, Reston, Va.; Kenneth Cooper, M.D.; Dan Green; Charles L. Sterling, Ed.D.; Robert Arnot, M.D.; Judy Young, NASPE; Dave Camione, University of Connecticut, Storrs; Hal Jordan, Manchester YMCA, Manchester, N.H.; John Cates, University of California, San Diego; Jackie Aher, illustrator; Michael Palgon, Editor, Bantam Doubleday Dell; David Seybold; Jillian Neal, My Gym, Santa Monica, Calif.; Betty Glass, Santa Monica Alternative Schoolhouse, Santa Monica, Calif.

FINALLY! A SERIES DEDICATED TO REVERSING THE DECLINE IN YOUTH FITNESS!

arnold's fitness for kids

Volume 1:
Ages Birth - 5

Volume 2:
Ages 6 - 10

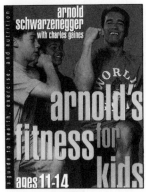

Volume 3:
Ages 11 - 14

DOUBLEDAY

Chairman of the President's Council on Physical Fitness and Sports

BY ARNOLD SCHWARZENEGGER

with CHARLES GAINES

The great majority of our kids are physically unfit. Here are some alarming statistics on the state of children's fitness today:

- **64% fail to meet minimum fitness standards**
- **obesity is up by 54%**
- **28% have high blood pressure**
- **almost 70% eat too much salt**
- **67% show risk factors for heart disease**

Fitness begins or doesn't begin at home. Parents everywhere must learn that teaching their children to be fit is just as important as teaching them to wear a seatbelt or to look both ways before crossing the street. And most importantly, parents have to learn that youth fitness is family fitness: that parents can join with their children to make fitness a fun, family adventure.

SO GET FIT WITH ARNOLD AND SAY "HASTA LA VISTA" TO POOR FITNESS FOREVER!

Collect the entire three volume set.

These three volumes are available at your local bookstore or if you would prefer to order direct, use this coupon form to order.

ISBN	TITLE	PRICE	X	QTY	=	TOTAL
42266-0	Arnold's Fitness for Kids, Vol. 1 Ages: Birth - 5	$15.00/$18.50 in Canada		____		_____
42267-9	Arnold's Fitness for Kids, Vol. 2 Ages: 6 - 10	$15.00/$18.50 in Canada		____		_____
42268-7	Arnold's Fitness for Kids, Vol. 3 Ages: 11 - 14	$15.00/$18.50 in Canada		____		_____

Shipping and handling (Add $2.50 per order) _____

TOTAL_____

Please send me the titles I have indicated above. I am enclosing $ _____. Send check or money order in U.S. funds only (no COD's or cash please). Please make check payable to Doubleday Consumer Services. Allow 4 - 6 weeks for delivery. Prices and availability are subject to change without notice.

Name_____

Address _____ Apt#_____

City _____ State _____ Zip _____

Send completed coupon and payment to:
Doubleday Consumer Services
Dept DR3
2451 South Wolf Road
Des Plaines, IL 60018

DR3/4-93